IMAGES
of England

GLOUCESTERSHIRE'S INDEPENDENT BUSES AND COACHES THE YEARS TO 1945

AJS Pilot DG 4390 was destined for Warner of Tewkesbury. It was photographed outside the Cheltenham premises of Tyler & Martin where its body was constructed, awaiting delivery in April 1932.

IMAGES
of England

GLOUCESTERSHIRE'S INDEPENDENT BUSES AND COACHES
THE YEARS TO 1945

Compiled by
Colin Martin

TEMPUS

First published 2000
Copyright © Colin Martin, 2000

Tempus Publishing Limited
The Mill, Brimscombe Port,
Stroud, Gloucestershire, GL5 2QG

ISBN 0 7524 1736 3

Typesetting and origination by
Tempus Publishing Limited
Printed in Great Britain by
Midway Clark Printing, Wiltshire

From 1932 until 1944, Percy Grindle's Forest Greyhound fleet included two of these Gilfords.
GJ 5770 was posed for this publicity shot in a typical Forest of Dean setting.

Contents

Acknowledgements

The photographs reproduced in this book have been collected over many years. I wish to express my gratitude to the following, all of whom have very willingly contributed photographs or information. Sadly a number of those acknowledged below, including several who were particularly enthusiastic about the eventual publication of this volume, will be unable to see its final form.

Mrs Atkins, Cam; Mr Ayland, Saul; Mr D. Bowles, Ford; Bristol Vintage Bus Group; Mr T. Challis, Cirencester; *The Citizen*, Gloucester; Mr E. Cooke, Northleach; Mr A. Cottrell, Mitcheldean; Mr B. Cox, Ellwood; Mr E. Cuss, Cirencester; Dean Heritage Centre; Mr A. Dingle, Quenington; Mr R. Duggan, Mitcheldean; Mr R.J. Edworthy, Rogiet; Mr V. Fluck, Stow-on-the-Wold; Mr S.J. Gardiner, France Lynch; Gloucester Folk Museum; *Gloucestershire Echo*; Gloucestershire Records Office; Mr Gray, Marlborough; Mr H. Grindle, Ruardean Hill; Mrs Hamblett, Gloucester; Mr C. Hancock, Gloucester; Mrs Huxley, South Cerney; Mrs I. Joiner, Hucclecote; Mr L. Leach, Frampton-on-Severn; Mr R. Marfell, Ruardean Woodside; Mr R. Marshall, Burnley; Mr D. Meek, Newent; Mr C. Miles, Guiting Power; Mr Mills, Gloucester; Mr J. Mudge, Worcester; Mr N. Meanwell, Cheltenham; Mrs E. Olivey, Cinderford; Mr F. Patterson, Gloucester; Mr D. Perry, Cinderford; Pulham's Coaches, Bourton-on-the-Water; Mr H.J. Roberts, Cinderford; Mr J. Russell, Wormington; Mrs B. Shaw, Arlingham; Mrs M. Simcock, Cheltenham; Mr R.H.G. Simpson, Oxford; J.C. Smith & Son Photography, Ledbury; Mr L. Tuffley, Mitcheldean; Mr Tyler, Cheltenham; Mr N.H. Warner, Westmancote; Mr A.M.R. Watts, Lydney.

In all cases all reasonable steps have been taken to ensure that permission has been obtained from appropriate copyright holders; my apologies to anyone whom I have been unable either to identify or to contact.

The forbearance and co-operation of my wife during my frequent absences, while photographs were being sourced and researches undertaken, is also acknowledged.

And finally an appeal. I will warmly welcome news of any more photographs of buses and coaches with Gloucestershire connections in order that my developing collection, and more importantly any future reference volumes, may represent as many aspects of the county's transport heritage as is possible.

Introduction

My awareness of the smaller bus and coach operators of Gloucestershire began to develop in the early 1960s, just as the last pre-war vehicles were disappearing from the county's roads. It is a sobering thought that the forty-year span of my personal interest represents the same interval of time as that covered by the period of rapid development which saw the primitive charabancs of the 1920s metamorphose into the very respectable vehicles of the 1960s. For although this volume begins with a summary of the main developments which had taken place late in the nineteenth century, the motor bus story, with which it is primarily concerned, really began to develop in the years immediately following the end of the First War. Although it was not apparent to me when my interest began, the 1960s were of course just another milestone on the journey of ongoing technological and automotive development; thus, by comparison with what we take as the norm today, those vehicles of forty years ago, which we thought at the time were the last word in comfort and refinement, would not in fact have been well equipped to cope with the road conditions and passenger expectations of this new century.

For those puzzled by the term 'independent' in the title of this publication, a few words of explanation may be helpful. Since the early days of the twentieth century, there have been both large and small players in what we today recognise as 'the bus industry'. In Gloucestershire the early major operators included the Bristol Tramways & Carriage Company, the Great Western Railway, and the National Omnibus and Transport Company (latterly, in this area, The Western National Omnibus Company). Another large business soon to evolve was Red and White, with its origins in the Gloucestershire town of Lydney. These larger company groupings, along with the urban transport systems in both Cheltenham and Gloucester, and the much-lamented Black & White Motorways of Cheltenham, are excluded from this record; most have indeed already been the subject of specific reference works and all, at various times, found themselves taken into state ownership. By contrast, this book presents a record of the vehicles operated by many of Gloucestershire's privately owned and generally small, often family-run, businesses.

There were many such operators across the county, with the majority based in the more rural areas. Some were determined not to progress beyond their initial vehicle, and indeed in some cases this was only in use for a matter of months, before being recognised as an uneconomic proposition. In other cases the early charabancs were sufficiently profitable for fleets of a dozen or so vehicles to be incrementally acquired, with their owners remaining in coaching for all of their working lives. This book outlines the development and early operations of those entrepreneurs whose vehicles are captured in this essentially photographic record. For every business mentioned, two or three more have been excluded through lack of suitable photographic records – or simply of space. In general terms, however, those recorded here are representative of the totality of the pre-war coaching pioneers across Gloucestershire.

Although some fifty-five years have elapsed since the newest of the vehicles depicted within these pages first took to the roads, a number of the operating concerns which the vehicles represent are still active on the county's transport scene today. For many operators coaching is a way of life and, in the case of a number of family concerns, successive generations have devoted their entire working lives to keeping the wheels turning.

This record is intended to appeal equally to those whose interests lie in either specific family businesses, the progressive development of the public transport scene, or consideration of how the developments in rural transport contributed to the wider tapestry of twentieth century social history. A few of the photographs 'rescued' during my researches had suffered a little over the years; in almost all cases they are, however, unique and are included here in order to present as comprehensive a review as is possible. Despite their condition I believe that their subjects will enhance, rather than detract from, the value of this publication. While this is essentially a record of developments within a single county, the account is generally representative of the progress made in many other areas of the UK, as the public enthusiastically embraced the possibilities of the motor vehicle.

Colin Martin, Woodmancote, January 2000

HOWSE'S MOTOR SERVICES,
ALDSWORTH.

BURFORD and CIRENCESTER.

		MONDAYS.		Fares.				WEDNESDAYS and FRIDAYS.		Fares.	
			a.m.	S.	R.				p.m.	S.	R.
Depart	BURFORD	....	10.0	1/6	2/6	Depart	BURFORD	....	12.0	1/6	2/6
„	ALDSWORTH	...	10.25	1/-	1/6	„	TAYNTON	....	12.10	1/3	2/-
„	BIBURY	....	10.35	1/-	1/6	„	BARRINGTON	...	12.20	1/3	2/-
	Arrive Cirencester 11.0 a.m.					„	WINDRUSH	......	12.30	1/3	2/-
						„	SHERBORNE	......	12.40	1/3	2/-
						„	ALDSWORTH	...	1.0	1/-	1/6
						„	BIBURY	....	1.15	1/-	1/6
							Arrive Cirencester 1.45 p.m.				

Depart Market-place 4.30 p.m. each day.

ALDSWORTH and CHELTENHAM.

	THURSDAYS.		Fares.	
		p.m.	S.	R.
Depart	ALDSWORTH	1.0	1/6	3/-
„	BARRINGTON	1.20	1/6	3/-
„	WINDRUSH	1.30	1/6	2/9
„	SHERBORNE	1.40	1/3	2/6
„	NORTHLEACH	1.55	1/3	2/6

Arrive Plough Yard, Cheltenham, 2.30 p.m.   Depart Plough Yard, 6.30 p.m.

14 and 20-SEATER SALOON BUSES FOR HIRE—MODERATE CHARGES.

Howse of Aldeworth first operated as a carrier with a horse-drawn van. This was replaced by a lorry bus in the 1920s, to be followed by the first buses later in that decade. The operation was therefore typical of many whose developments are outlined in this volume.

One
Horse Buses and Carriers' Carts

The use of horse power in its literal sense, for long distance coaching, had developed rapidly during the first half of the eighteenth century, but one hundred years later was in sharp decline as the railway network became firmly established throughout the land. Developments in Gloucestershire were in line with this national trend and the county's principal urban centres had all been connected to the main railway network by 1850. As responsibility for the carriage of mail was transferred to the railway companies and passengers were to appreciate the greater speed, comfort and general convenience of rail travel, long-distance horse-drawn road coaches had few advantages left to offer and soon disappeared from the scene at both national and local levels. At the same time, however, the use of the horse as a provider of more local public transport was becoming rather better organised, in part because of the opportunities for providing services to connect with the trains at some of the newly-opened stations.

Horse buses employed on localised services took various forms, according to the nature of the local requirement and the operating environment. In the larger towns the typical vehicle consisted of an enclosed saloon, accessed from the rear, and generally with three or four windows along its sides; additional seats on an open upper deck, were reached by a curving rear staircase. In smaller towns, the vehicles required less carrying capacity and a smaller saloon, with no upper deck, was quite adequate to meet the local needs. Open brakes were also available for private hire; in some cases (and Gloucester and Stroud are local examples) these were also used on local services – but generally only in the summer months, as they offered little protection from the elements. But on the rural services, with which this volume is primarily concerned, horse buses generally came in the form of carriers' carts.

While there is room for debate as to whether carriers' carts were buses at all, they offered those in rural areas the opportunity to travel into neighbouring towns and villages, generally at predetermined times each week. These carts effectively complemented the rail network, often serving those villages, hamlets and isolated farms not within easy reach of a railway station. While the fares were rather lower than those of the railways, they offered little in the way of comfort, and speed was influenced by a variety of factors, including the fitness of both the road surfaces and the horses, and the prevailing weather conditions. Carriers' carts varied considerably in their form and sophistication; some were no more than farm wagons fitted with rudimentary hoods, while others were custom-built. While some provided basic seating, the majority simply took the form of an enclosed van with passengers having to find the least uncomfortable perch on or between the variety of items typically found on board; not uncommonly the loads included smaller items of livestock travelling to or from the local market. The word 'bus' comes from the Latin *omnibus*, meaning 'for all'. This would dispel any doubts about such vehicles being categorised as buses.

Gloucestershire was served by an impressive network of carrier's services – Figures 1 and 2 summarise the advertised carriers' services running into both Cheltenham and Gloucester in 1919. Rather curiously the directories which publicized such services make scant reference to the omnibus services of the day. It may have been that there was little confidence that these would continue for any length of time, unfortunate experiences with early steam and motor vehicles, and then the curtailment of some such services during the war years having been fresh in the minds of all at that time. Experience, incidentally, has shown that the information within such directories is neither as complete nor as up-to-date as the publishers may have claimed; nevertheless a good impression may be gained of the general scene of the time.

Two features of carrier operations will be apparent from a perusal of the tables. There is a marked concentration of services on certain days of the week. These were of course the days on which the markets were held in each of the two larger towns, the markets being the main reason for country dwellers to travel into town, both to buy and to sell. Such local traditions can become very firmly rooted and even today a few additional services continue to run into Cheltenham from rural areas on Thursdays – even though the market has long gone! The second point of note is the use of inns as the departure points for all services; the inn yards would normally have provided facilities for the horses to be fed, watered and rested. Several of the inns had of course also provided similar facilities and, in some cases, overnight stabling for horses used on long-distance coaching services.

Scheduled Carriers' Services From Cheltenham in 1919 (Figure 1)

Operator,	Destination(s),	Days of Operation,	Boarding Point
Beasley	Beckford and Dumbleton	Thur, Sat	Royal
Booth,	Colesborne & North Cerney	Thur, Sat	Crown
Carpenter	Brockhampton	Tues, Thur, Sat	Plough
Cripps	Birdlip and Brimpsfield	Sat	Royal
Gardner**	Winchcombe	Daily	Crown
Green	Tewkesbury	Thur	Crown
Harvey	Alderton	Thur	Crown
Haynes	Cleeve	Tues, Thur & Sat	Lamb
Holder	Gotherington & Oxenton	Thur & Sat	Lamb
Hunt	Colesborne	Thur	Plough
Lockey	Hasleton	Thur	Dove and Rainbow
Midwinter	Withington	Tues & Sat	Crown
Miles	Dowdeswell, Andoversford, Hampen, Hawling Guiting and Kineton,	Tues, Thur & Sat	Crown
Newcomb	Birdlip	Fri	Royal
Perrett	Shipton Oliffe	Tues, Thur & Sat	Crown
Pulham	Dowdeswell, Andoversford, Naunton & Bourton-on-the-Water	Thur & Sat	Crown
Ryman	Lower Guiting	Tues, Thur & Sat	Royal
Stevens	Dowdeswell	Tues, Thur & Sat	Old Swan
Watton	Birdlip	Tues & Sat	Royal
West	Sheepscombe	Thur	Royal
Williams	Brockhampton	Tues, Thur & Sat	Old Swan
Wright	Cutsdean & Didbrook	Thur & Sat	Crown

** The Gardner service was specifically identified as an 'omnibus service' while the remainder were all categorised as carriers. Gardner is known to have been using a horse brake on the service at that time.

Scheduled Carriers' Services From Gloucester in 1919 (Figure 2)

Operator	Destination(s)	Days of Operation,	Boarding Point
Ayland	Westbury-on-Severn	Mon, Wed & Sat	White Swan
Barnes	May Hill	Mon, Wed & Sat	Saracen's Head
Bartlett	Blaisdon & Longhope	Sat	Old Dial
Bowers	Staunton	Sat	Old Dial
Brown	Cheltenham	Daily	Welsh Harp
Bullock	Longhope	Wed & Sat	Saracen's Head
Dangerfield	Stonehouse	Daily	Albion
Davis	Newent	Wed & Fri	Booth Hall
Dring	Redmarley	Mon, Wed & Sat	Old Dial
Field	Redmarley	Mon, Wed, & Sat	Old Dial
Fluck	Taynton & Tibberton	Wed & Sat	Anchor
Fryer	Epney, Framilode, Fretherne	Mon, Wed & Sat	Albion
Gardner	Huntley	Sat	Anchor
Green	Tewkesbury	Wed & Sat	Spread Eagle
Hanks	Painswick	Mon, Wed, Fri & Sat	Saracen's Head
Jones	Cambridge & Slimbridge	Sat	Talbot
Jones	Upleadon	Mon, Wed & Sat	Duke of Sussex
Knight	Elmore, Epney & Longney	Mon, Wed, & Sat	Talbot
Poole	Huntley	Sat	Old Dial
Smith	Longney	Mon, Wed & Sat	Talbot
Taylor	Staunton	Mon, Tues, Wed, Fri & Sat	Old Dial
Walkley	Cinderford	Mon, Wed & Sat	Saracen's Head
Watkins	Pendock & Redmarley	Mon, Wed & Sat	Old Dial
White	Stroud	Mon, Wed & Sat	Talbot
Wilce	Tirley	Mon, Wed & Sat	Spread Eagle

Several of the coach companies still operating today can trace their roots directly to nineteenth century carriers' operations. Pulham's (then of Naunton, but now of Bourton-on-the-Water) and Cottrell's of Mitcheldean were both operating as rural carriers in the 1880s, into Cheltenham and Gloucester. Perrett's Coaches of Shipton Oliffe can trace its origins to Mr Makepeace's carrier's cart, which ran thrice weekly between Andoversford and Cheltenham. Pulham's, Cottrell's and Perrett's now operate six days a week, over the same routes. The Castleways coach business in Winchcombe is largely built on the horse bus services established by the Gardner family between Winchcombe and Cheltenham. Mr Gardner sold out to Mr W.R. Gillett, who introduced motor buses in the 1920s. The business was sold to Castleways by Mr Gillett's son, on his retirement in 1971.

While horse bus services in towns had started to be replaced by tramcars and early motor buses around the start of the twentieth century, carrier's carts remained an important feature of rural life until the 1920s, when the rapid spread of motor buses, offering more frequent, more rapid and more comfortable journeys into town, rendered them largely redundant. Also, local tradesmen, some returning from the First World War where they had their first real experiences of motor traction, started to use motor vehicles for the collection and delivery of goods and livestock. Rural buses just carried passengers and a small number of parcels, in effect reversing the needs of previous decades.

However, several horse drawn carriers managed to survive into the 1930s. One of the last in the area was Mrs Chandler of Great Washbourne who made the last journey with her horse-drawn van from Dumbleton into Cheltenham in October 1937. She had made the weekly journey for twenty-two years like her mother and her grandmother before. It does, however, seem unlikely that passengers to the end, as regular motor bus services were brought in for the Gloucestershire/Worcestershire border area, as in most others, in the 1920s.

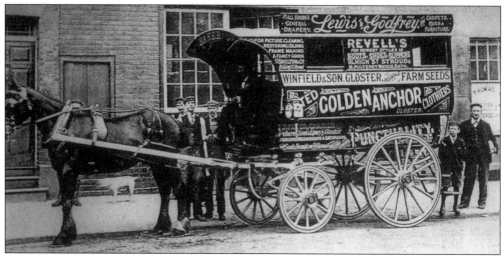

This wonderfully ornate vehicle was a carrier's van built to the requirements of its operator, a Mr Fryer. Every inch of the vehicle is covered with elaborate signwriting, either advertising local traders or giving details of the vehicle's weekly services. They operated along the course of the Severn from Fretherne, Saul and Epney into Gloucester on Mondays, Wednesdays and Saturdays, and from Saul and Frampton-on-Severn eastwards to Stroud on Tuesdays and Fridays. The vehicle appears to be known as *Punctuality*, an attribute of his operation which Mr Fryer clearly regarded as important to his customers. The vehicle looks immaculate and the picture may have been taken as it was leaving its builder's works. Two horses would almost certainly have been required when the vehicle was laden.

Believed to be the vehicle with which Mr W.E. Pulham started in business in 1880, this carrier's cart is seen while on its rounds in the Cotswolds. The vehicle trundled from villages surrounding Mr Pulham's home in Naunton into Cheltenham twice a week, while on other days it served the local farming communities nearer to its home. Bourton-on-the-Water and Upper and Lower Slaughters are specifically mentioned in its signwriting.

More typical of urban horse buses, but here deployed on a distinctly rural service, is this two-horse bus of George Symonds. Symonds' vehicles maintained regular services within Gloucester's urban confines, but this rural route left the City streets some four miles behind and ventured northwards through Longford and Twigworth to Norton. Note the name *Pioneer* on the sides of the vehicle and the identification of Symonds as a Jobmaster based at College Mews. The curving staircase at the rear of the bus is clearly visible, as is a tantalising assortment of jars in the windows of Norton Post Office outside which the vehicle was photographed.

This small horse brake with inward facing longitudinal seats was used by Mr W.R. Gillett of Winchcombe to link Cheltenham and Winchcombe in the early twentieth century. The route went over the top of Cleeve Hill, more than justifying the provision of two horses. Passengers were requested to alight for the steepest part of the climb over the hill, those opting to stay on board paying a surcharge of 3d on top of the 1s basic fare. Winchcombe's link with Cheltenham, six miles distant, was not operational until 1906. However, the bus service continued to thrive. There is still a daily service today.(Photo: *Gloucestershire Echo*)

This brake, named *The Comet*, was photographed in Abbey Terrace, Winchcombe in August 1911; as far as is known this vehicle was used only for private parties, and not to operate any regular services. Four horses were in harness on this occasion, almost certainly because the party had travelled over Cleeve Hill. The passengers were all members of the Gloucestershire Root, Fruit and Grain Society *en route* to their annual field day, held that year at Winchcombe's Sudeley Castle. (Photo: *Gloucestershire Echo*)

These two horse brakes were about to take members of the Institute of Water Engineers from their annual conference in Cheltenham to visit Witcombe Waterworks, some five miles distant. The photograph was taken outside the Queen's Hotel in June 1912. Note that the leading brake has inward facing longitudinal seats, while that behind, with its canopy in place, has transverse seating. Upholstery appears to be non-existent – such brakes generally offered a degree of comfort suitable only for short journeys. Those illustrated appear to seat about twenty. Only three ladies are visible in the group, others' wives had probably decided that Cheltenham's shops were a better place to spend an afternoon than the water treatment works! (Photo: *Gloucestershire Echo*)

Two

Experiments with Steam Propulsion

Steam-powered road coaches first appeared in the country in the 1820s. The public was never at ease with steam propulsion being harnessed in this way; the potential speed of the vehicles and the fears of boiler explosions produced a significant body of opposition. Organised lobbying resulted in the introduction of a range of financial deterrents, including increased turnpike charges and the imposition of hefty penalties for any coach caught exceeding the prevailing legal limit of 4mph. Although tried in various parts of the UK, on both local and long-distance routes, the financial impediments ensured that each such experiment was short-lived. Locally, in February 1831, Sir Charles Dance put a steam carriage, built by Goldsworthy Gurney, into service between Cheltenham and Gloucester. Although the service over the nine mile route attracted several thousand passengers during its few weeks of operation, the venture met with the same degree of opposition as those in other areas and was quickly withdrawn.

It was on the road between Cirencester and Fairford that steam propulsion was later to reappear. Although a horse bus service ran between the two towns, there was an awareness of the benefit that a railway link could bring to the area. The first step towards improving the service, and perhaps to demonstrate more clearly the potential support for construction of a rail line, was the arrival in 1897 of a steam tractor with a twenty-seat passenger trailer. This ungainly vehicle operated over the ten-mile route during the summer months of 1898 and 1899, but was not a success and can have done little good for the cause of the railway lobbyists. In the end, the railway never came.

Five years were to pass before further steam-propelled omnibuses appeared on the same road, running on to Lechlade, some three miles beyond Fairford. Two paraffin-burning steam buses, built in Chelmsford by the Clarkson company, were registered in May 1904 to Mr Ernest Nash in Cheltenham. The operation was, however, centred in Lechlade, to where it is believed Mr Nash relocated at about that time. Mr Nash traded as the Cirencester & District Motor Omnibus Company and the service ran twice a day on six days of the week. The two Clarksons were allocated registration numbers, AD 303 and 304, by Gloucestershire County Council's licensing office, vehicle licensing having been introduced across the country at the start of that year. Interestingly, while still in Lechlade, the Nash brothers acquired another Clarkson chassis. The registration AD 805 was obtained, but at the time of the initial declaration in 1906 the motor taxation ledgers reveal that it carried no body. It has not been established whether this became a third local steam bus or whether the chassis was sold on for use elsewhere.

Ernest Nash moved to Devon with his brother Arthur in the early months of 1907, taking the vehicles with him to form the basis of a new venture, the Paignton & District Motor Omnibus Co. One of his colleagues there was a Mr Frank Young. Competition with the bus service operated in Paignton by the Great Western Railway soon led to the smaller concern selling out to the railway company. As the dust began to settle on initial forays into motor bus operation, takeovers and consolidation became inevitable. This helped to release vehicles onto the second-hand market, where many were snapped up by other entrepreneurs keen to exploit their potential elsewhere. Thus, Mr Young bought two Clarksons, at least one of which had itself seen service with the GWR at one of its increasing number of bus-operating locations, and moved to Lechlade, re-establishing steam bus operation between that town and Cirencester. Yet this was to be an even shorter-lived venture than that of its predecessor and ceased during 1909. It seems likely that Mr Young then experimented with a motor bus, as a small vehicle of that description, registered AD 1326 and rated at 12hp, but of unknown make, was licensed to him in May 1909.

Following Mr Young's worthy but seemingly unsuccessful initiatives, the horse bus service continued until Norton Brothers of Lechlade introduced motor buses on the route in 1921. Frank Young, meanwhile, went on to establish a garage in Lechlade and ran it until he sold out in 1959. Although not directly a part of the Gloucestershire story, it is interesting to note that the Nash brothers were not deterred by the short lived ventures at Lechlade or Paignton; following the sale of their operation in Devon they took at least one of their Clarkson vehicles to start a new venture in Leicester.

While the choice of the Gloucester to Cheltenham road for the 1831 experiments might have been reasonably predictable, given that these were (and indeed still are) the largest towns in the area and that the road between them involved no gradients, it is rather curious that the Cirencester-Fairford road should have been the setting for all three of the later attempts to establish steam bus operation in the county.

Although steam was a popular form of propulsion for heavy goods vehicles until well into the 1930s, this was not the case for their passenger-carrying equivalents. At the same time as these steam experiments were taking place, the popularity of petrol-engined vehicles was steadily increasing. Chapter 4 records their early days upon Gloucestershire's roads.

Vehicle Registration in Gloucestershire

In January 1904 motor vehicles were allocated identification numbers, which we refer to now as registration numbers. Many of the vehicles illustrated in this volume carry Gloucestershire registrations and a brief outline of their progression may assist those not familiar with the system to follow the chronology.

With effect from 1904 each County and County Borough Council became responsible for managing vehicle licensing within their local areas. To start the system each such issuing authority was allocated one or more identification letters (or more usually digraphs) which would then be applied along with a serial number to each vehicle. Gloucestershire County Council was allocated digraph AD and thus the first number it issued was AD 1. Until 1920 numbers were reused once a vehicle had been scrapped or sold to an owner outside the area, as vehicles were often re-registered when moving to another county. Thus for numbers up to approximately AD 8000 there may have been several vehicles which at different times carried the same registration mark. Thereafter vehicles were not normally re-registered and numbers not reused.

Gloucestershire reached AD 9999 in October 1921; its next digraph was DD and numbers DD 1-9999 were issued between 1921 and June 1926. This was followed by DF (June 1926-April 1930) and DG (April 1930-September 1934).

Three letter marks commenced with AAD in September 1934, followed by ADD, ADF and ADG. BAD commenced in December 1935 and at the outbreak of World War II EAD was nearing completion. Progress slowed very considerably during the war years and FDD was the current mark in 1945.

The earliest buses registered in Gloucestershire are believed to have been motor bus AD 301 and steam buses AD 303 and 304 of Ernest Nash, all registered in May 1904.

As a County Borough, Gloucester City operated independently of the county, and had a single digraph, FH. FH 9999 was issued in the spring of 1936, followed by AFH 1. CFH was nearing completion in 1939 and peace had returned before DFH had been exhausted.

The earliest FH registrations traced to buses are FH 66, a 1907 Dennis, and 1909 Wolseley FH 96, although they only became passenger carriers later in their lives.

This is the vehicle which operated experimentally over the ten-mile route between Cirencester and Fairford in 1898 and 1899. The vehicle was not a success, largely due to lack of traction; its narrow wheels were unable to establish a sufficiently firm grip on the variable road surfaces. In order to minimise problems the vehicle was used only in the summer months. Known as a LIFU, an acronym of its makers, the Liquid Fuel Engineering Company, this oil-burning steam-driven contraption had been constructed in the Isle of Wight and consisted of a towing tractor coupled to a four-wheeled twenty-seat passenger carriage. The tractor itself contained a goods and parcels compartment. Note the absence of a registration number – the vehicle pre-dated the introduction of such numbers by several years. It is understood that several similar vehicles were produced for use at other locations, but all suffered from the same difficulties. As noted above, those lobbying for the construction of a railway link between the two towns had hoped that the operation and performance of this vehicle would have strengthened their case. In the event the two towns never were connected by rail, although both were well served by Great Western Railway branch lines, with Cirencester additionally having a station (Watermoor) on the Midland and South Western Junction Railway, with trains running regularly between Southampton and Cheltenham.

The novelty of the Clarkson steam buses operating between Cirencester and Lechlade was such that they featured in a number of contemporary commercial viewcards. The three views on these pages all depict Ernest Nash's two original vehicles, registered AD 303 and 304. The George Hotel in Fairford provided the backcloth to the view above. Note the provision of a longitudinal bench seat on the roof, arguably making the vehicle a double-decker! At least one large suitcase may also be seen on the vehicle's roof with the owner's initials, M.R.Y., clearly visible; it seems likely that at least one of the passengers was therefore using this bus to connect with a train. The driver looks very smartly attired in what appears to be a leather jacket, while his conductor is wearing his cash pouch and ticket rack. The chain drive to the vehicle's solid-tyred rear wheels is clearly visible.

One of the Nash vehicles is seen in Lechlade when the service was first launched in 1904, waiting to make the thirteen mile trip to Cirencester. (Photo: *Gloucestershire Echo*)

Cirencester Market Place has always been a popular place for photography, and one of Nash's Clarkson steam buses provides added interest in this view. The vehicles were sometimes referred to as Chelmsford steamers. The fleet-name Cirencester & District Motor Omnibus Co was used on these vehicles – which may have implied that the Nash brothers had intended to develop a network of services in the area, but that was not to be.

This vehicle was one of the two Clarksons subsequently acquired by Mr Frank Young. It had originated with the Great Western Railway, which had commenced bus operations at many locations throughout its operating areas in England and Wales. Its GWR origins are confirmed by the small rectangular plate affixed to its waistrail behind the driver's compartment; these plates were a feature of all GWR buses and carried the vehicle's fleet-number. This vehicle is believed to have been registered DA 81 and was broadly similar to the earlier Nash vehicles. However, the body sides extend further to the rear of the vehicle, enclosing the boarding platform – on the similar Nash vehicles the platforms were open to the elements. On the Young vehicle the bonnet sides have smooth panelling with decorative lining, while the Nash vehicles have louvred panels. DA registrations were issued by Wolverhampton and the vehicle had therefore perhaps been initially deployed by the GWR in the western Midlands.

TIME TABLE.
❀

Mondays only.

	a.m.	p.m.			a.m.	p.m.
Leachlade	· 9.50	1.40	|	Cirencester	· 12.0	5.30
Fairford	· 10.30	2.5	|	Fairford	· 12.50	6.15
Cirencester	· 11.30	2.55	|	Lechlade	· 1.20	6.55

Thursdays only.

Leachlade	7.45		5.50	Cirencester	9.15	1.45	8.0
Fairford	8.10	10.30	6.10	Fairford	10.5	2.30	8.45
Cirencester	9.0	11.30	7.0	Leachlade	...	3.5	9.10

Week Days, except Mons and Thurs.

Leachlade	· 9.50	2.25	Cirencester	· 12.10	5.20
Fairford	· 10.30	3.0	Fairford	· 12.50	6.15
Cirencester	· 11.30	3.45	Lechlade	· 1.35	6.55

Any further information may be obtained from the Manager, Riverside, Lechlade.

This early timetable for the steam bus service between Cirencester and Lechlade is believed to relate to the period of operation by Mr Young. Note the variable spelling of Lechlade!

Three

Lorry Buses

While some early buses were little more than crudely converted lorries, the term 'lorry buses' is generally applied to vehicles which were specifically intended to serve both as lorries and buses, but, unlike carriers' carts, not necessarily at the same time. In some cases they were open trucks onto which bench seats could be fitted, as and when the vehicles were required to carry passengers; tilts of varying sophistication were generally added to provide some protection from the elements. In other cases enclosed cabins, complete with seats, were lifted onto the beds of the wagons and anchored in place.

An alternative to the lorry-bus was the 'convertible', where a chassis had two (or more) completely independent bodies which could quickly be exchanged to meet the needs of the day. In these cases the bus bodies were generally more elaborate than those found on lorry-buses. When carrying their bus or charabanc bodies, the vehicles were in effect indistinguishable from their fixed-body counterparts.

In Gloucestershire, lorry buses continued to operate, albeit in small numbers, until after the Second World War. Most of the local examples were operated in the Forest of Dean; their primary function was the transportation of miners to the various collieries scattered throughout the area. During the day, the seats and/or cabins were removed and the vehicles were used to deliver coal, or for more general haulage work. Lorry buses were also found in the larger towns and Cheltenham and Gloucester both had examples. However, these were not used to provide regular services, but, in their bus guise, were used primarily by sports teams for travel to their weekend fixtures. During the week the vehicles carried out general haulage duties.

An early lorry bus was this Ford Model T – in fact an extended wheelbase version known as the TT. DD 116 was delivered to Mr John Merritt of Minchinhampton in November 1921. Although it has been said to be an ex-military truck, the chassis number, available from the wealth of motor taxation information held by Gloucestershire Records Office, indicates that it was in fact a new delivery. The body has low wooden sides, surmounted by a canvas tilt. The rear ends of the longitudinal benches are just visible in this view. The two steps at the rear would require a fair degree of physical fitness – a marked contrast to the low floor, easy-access buses appearing in large numbers some eighty years later. Mr Merritt was to introduce several services in the Avening, Minchinhampton and Stroud area. These services, along with those of several other bus pioneers in the Stroud valleys, eventually found themselves in the hands of Red and White Services, following a series of mergers and take-overs. Red and White maintained a depot in Stroud for some twenty years – see Chapter 4.

Another Ford Model T was this December 1924 delivery to Mr Albert Meek of Nailbridge. DD 5960 was Mr Meek's first bus and it was used to inaugurate a service from Ruardean to Cinderford. When not so deployed the cabin was removed and the vehicle undertook general haulage work. Like most vehicles of its day, the Ford T's cab doors were unglazed; journeys of any length could therefore have been more than a little uncomfortable for the driver, particularly in the winter months. Nevertheless the windscreen and general structure of the cab provided much more protection for the driver than horse-drawn conveyances. Many of the photographs in this book were taken either when vehicles were newly delivered, or when they were in use on special occasions. In this case the vehicle appears to have been brand new. Note the small oval windows at the sides and rear of the cab; these were a not unusual feature of light commercial vehicles of the time. Mr Meek had been employed on the screens at Waterloo Colliery before investing in this vehicle. It is believed that this vehicle remained little more than a year with Meek, as its success resulted in it being traded-in in 1926 for a more conventional bus.

An example of a lorry bus which operated in a rather more urban area is this 1926 Morris Commercial T-type truck, placed in service by Mr C.H. Smith of Churchdown. Although still owned by Mr Smith's family, the Morris has been on display in the Gloucester Transport Museum for many years and may be inspected by making an appointment at the the nearby Folk Museum. The vehicl, as restored, lacks its drop-sides and additional seats, but still displays its Hackney Carriage plate to show that its use for carrying fourteen passengers had been approved by the local authority. It is known to have carried parties as far afield as Weston-Super-Mare. Although one or two passengers may have been accommodated alongside the driver in his cab, the bed of the vehicle looks very small for accommodating the remaining dozen travellers – hold very tight, please! In these views (above and opposite) the vehicle is seen within the museum, surrounded by a variety of smaller exhibits. Although the Morris has not ventured out of the museum for very many years, it successfully completed the London-Brighton vintage vehicle run during the 1960s. The vehicle was not licensed as a Public Service Vehicle once the 1930 Road Traffic Act had been implemented and was thereafter used for local haulage and agricultural work; it remained active until the 1950s. The T was the first Morris Commercial truck, introduced in 1924, the T signifying 'Tonner' – one ton carrying capacity.

Many local vehicles, both passenger and goods, had their bodies constructed by Healey's of Gloucester, at their works near Westgate Bridge. Healey's products normally carried the coachbuilder's identity stamped on metal plates, such as this fixed to the framing at the base of the cab doors, on the above vehicle.

Another view of the Morris T in Gloucester Transport Museum. The museum also houses the partly restored body of a horse-drawn Gloucester tramcar.

When Public Service Vehicle licensing was introduced in 1931, R.A. Lister, the Dursley engineering firm, declared five of its vehicles as PSVs. It is assumed that these were lorries used for staff transport, the PSV status suggesting that fares were charged. The newest of the vehicles was Morris Z DF 3884, dating from 1927. Morris had introduced the Z in 1926 as a 24/30cwt vehicle to extend the Morris Commercial range above the one ton limit of the T model. Interestingly, the vehicle is seen here laden with floral tributes and heading the funeral cortege for Sir Ashton Lister through Dursley on 9 December 1929. Lorry buses certainly led a varied life! (Photo: *Gloucestershire Echo*)

Mr Archibald Russell of Wormington placed this Chevrolet X lorry bus in service in April 1926. It was supplied by Goodalls of Evesham. The vehicle, registered DD 9472, was used to provide a service from Wormington into Evesham, via Aston Somerville, and is seen here in Wormington village. Many early providers of rural bus services had other business interests; indeed the only way many could justify the purchase and running costs of a vehicle was to make it available for a variety of purposes. Thus, Mr Russell used this Chevrolet to support his own farming activities, in addition to undertaking haulage work for others in the area and for its regular passenger carrying activities. A further Chevrolet lorry bus joined the fleet in 1930. While they may have looked a little primitive, both Chevrolets are understood to have undertaken long journeys, and like the Morris on the previous page, are known to have reached Weston-Super-Mare, some eighty miles from Wormington. The tilt on this vehicle had been built in Goodall's own body shop. Many garages at that time continued to offer a much wider range of services than those directly related to vehicle repair and maintenance; indeed many of the rural garage businesses had developed from village smithies, accustomed to turning their hands to a wide variety of engineering tasks. The photograph is sufficiently clear for the build quality of Goodall's work to be seen.

Russell's Chevrolet DD 9472 features again in these two views; that above was also taken in Wormington while the view below captured the vehicle in the open countryside. Note that on the near-side of the vehicle the Russell business is described as 'Market Gardeners, Carriers and Hauliers' while on the off-side it is styled 'Fruit Merchants, Carriers and Hauliers'.

By 1936, Mr Frederick Russell had joined his father in the business. However, Mr Russell senior was insistent that their next vehicle would also be a lorry bus, although most local service providers had by then purchased more conventional buses. The growth in demand for rural transport was such that passenger and goods vehicles could now co-exist with generally sufficient work to keep both types fully occupied. Unusually, however, Mr Russell preferred to retain the flexibility which the dual purpose vehicle provided. It appears that his adherence to the lorry bus design was no deterrent to private party bookings. The 1936 purchase was this Bedford 30cwt WS, which was delivered by Goodalls in May of that year. BDD 218 was licensed to carry twelve passengers. It is seen here on the Russell farm with its tilt removed, and a good load of hay on board. The guard rails running between the wheels offer clear confirmation that it had been modified to conform with PSV requirements. The tall headboard behind the cab is also visible; this provided support for the forward end of the tilt body which once again had been built by Goodalls. The WS had been introduced in 1932, but by 1936 it had already been significantly restyled; the front axle was now set back and the cab had altogether a more modern appearance.

DF 7717 was the earliest of five buses known to have been operated by A and I Marfell, trading as Marfell Bros, of Ruardean Woodside. It was a Chevrolet LQ, delivered in May 1929 and is thought to have been the only lorry bus in the Marfell fleet, subsequent vehicles having been fitted with more conventional bus or coach bodies. The Chevrolet was normally used on the service from Woodside through Brierley, Nailbridge, Drybrook and Ruardean to Waterloo Colliery at Lydbrook. Another member of the Marfell family, H.M. Marfell, also from Ruardean Woodside, was running a quite separate bus operation in the late 1920s and through the following decade. The Chevrolet 30cwt range was very popular throughout the country in the 1920s for both goods and passenger applications, but the marque was to give way to the Bedford range in 1931. Many of the photographs in this book were not intended to be views of the buses at all – but of the parties they were carrying, or the events they were attending. In this case it is likely that the children in their party frocks sitting on the Chevrolet's running board were the main attraction for the photographer.

Mr William Huxley ran the George Inn and also a local garage business in South Cerney. He commenced operation of a daily service from the village into Cirencester via Siddington in the late 1920s, using this small truck with a canvas hood. Note that two transparent panels are included in the sides of the hood to let in a little extra light. When photographed the vehicle was bedecked with flowers and placards for a local celebration, to say nothing of the beer barrels being secured on top of the canvas tilt! No further details of the vehicle have been ascertained.

This is really a 'van bus', not a lorry bus, but the principle is the same – the vehicle fulfils two roles. Or in this case perhaps 'rolls', as it was operated by Mr Gearing, the village baker at Ampney Crucis. In between bakery deliveries, the bus ran a service from its home village to Cirencester. Here it appears to have taken the local scouts on an outing. It is thought that the vehicle was a 1920s Chevrolet. Mr Gearing died in 1932 and his bus operation ceased, his son concentrating on the bakery business. This is thought to have been the only 'bus' Mr Gearing had operated.

Pneumatic tyres were fitted all round on this early 1930s lorry bus. The vehicle is seen at the Cheltenham coachworks of Tyler and Martin. Although destined for use in the Forest of Dean, the actual purchaser is not known. As with the Meek and Marfell examples it again takes the form of a cabin bolted on to a dropside truck. The chassis is a Ford AA, the single rear wheels indicating that this was a 30cwt model. Note the guard rails running along the sides of the chassis between the wheels, by then a requirement for Public Service Vehicles. The cabins on some of these earlier lorry buses were unglazed; the view was presumably taken that glazing was unnecessary for the short daily journeys they were normally required to undertake, although those travelling to the coast or other more distant locations may quickly have reached other conclusions. In practical terms however, as the cabins were regularly mounted and demounted, the flexing of the less robust bodies would undoubtedly have caused problems should fixed glazing have been fitted, and there was also a need to minimise weight for handling purposes. In this case however, despite its utilitarian appearance, the cabin looks particularly solid and has the luxury of sliding side windows. Despite continuing healthy sales, Ford had realised in the mid-1920s that the Model T was in need of replacement. Production therefore ceased early in 1927, although its replacement, the A range, was not launched until later that year. The first examples of the A appeared in the UK in 1928. The A itself provided a car and light van chassis, with the AA being the more robust 30cwt model on a longer wheel base goods chassis; two ton variants were also available. Ford introduced the BB as the successor to the AA late in 1932, although 30cwt AAs continued to appear as the basis of fourteen-seat PSVs until 1935.

31

CDD 361 was one of the later generation of lorry buses and was based on a Ford BBE chassis. It was new in July 1937 to Mr B.H. Cecil of Clement Ends. Standing alongside the vehicle is Mr Reg Cox; his brother M.J. Cox of Ellwood had bought the Ford in 1939 and operated it until 1948. In addition to transporting miners, and for local coal delivery duties between their shift changes, Mr Cox used the Ford to transport working parties of Prisoners of War during World War II. This wartime photograph could equally well have been included in Chapter 5; the vehicle has its headlight mask in place and has its bumper and the edges of its wings and body picked out in white paint in the hope of improving its visibility during blackout periods. Both Cecil and Cox families continue in the transport business today, although neither has been involved in coaching for many years. The B.H. Cecil name lives on in the haulage operations now centred on Blakeney, while Brian Cox continues his fathers garage business in Ellwood. The BBE was the semi-forward control model in Ford's 'B' range.

Four

Motor Buses
1904-1940

Mainstream motor buses need rather less in the way of introduction than the alternatives and variants so far outlined; it is however interesting to reflect on how, in one particular respect, developments have almost come full circle over the past seventy years. Once motor bus production began to settle down in the 1920s, many of the rural vehicles were built upon Ford Model T or Chevrolet 30cwt chassis, as has already been demonstrated in Chapter 3; more examples of both appear in the following pages. Neither had specifically been designed for use as the underframe of a bus or coach; the Ford T was essentially a car chassis, but found itself used for every conceivable vehicular purpose, while the Chevrolet chassis was primarily intended to carry goods bodywork. Both, however, performed well as the basis of charabancs, buses and coaches, generally seating fourteen passengers in relative comfort.

Over the years the seating capacities of single-deck buses gradually increased to reach upwards of fifty seats in the twelve-metre long vehicles of the 1980s. Such vehicles were almost invariably constructed upon specifically designed passenger chassis. In that same decade, however, operators of many services, both urban and rural, faced up to the decline in passenger numbers, by moving, quite dramatically in some cases, to small capacity vehicles, generally seating between sixteen and twenty-five. As with their more distant forebears, the bodies for these vehicles were usually mounted on goods vehicle chassis, one of the more popular choices once again coming from the Ford range – this time in the form of the ubiquitous multi-purpose Transit.

This chapter explores the progressive development of motor buses owned by Gloucestershire's independent operators during the first four decades of the twentieth century. While it does not delve into the technicalities, the increasing sophistication and comfort provided by both body and chassis design will be readily apparent. One of the biggest advances was of course the move to pneumatic tyres during the 1920s; by the end of that decade most vehicles had fully enclosed bodywork, although sliding 'sunshine' roofs remained very popular on coaches. These improvements in passenger comfort were quickly followed by the implementation of the Road Traffic Act of 1930, which formally introduced the category of Public Service Vehicle, and set out formal licensing procedures for all such vehicles and the services on which they were operated. The 1930s also marked the introduction of much more stringent controls over PSV design and construction. One of the effects of this new legislative framework was the disappearance from the scene of some of the more primitive vehicles hitherto in use on the county's roads, and the loss of some of the less conventional pioneers, as a greater degree of professionalism and standardization was introduced to the industry.

While at the beginning of the period under review the typical vehicle seated fourteen, by the 1940s new vehicles generally provided thirty or more seats within the then maximum permitted legal length of 27ft 6ins for a two-axle single-decker. Many of the larger operating concerns had begun to specify diesel engines in their new vehicles during the 1930s, but petrol engines remained the norm with smaller operators until the late 1950s. Bedford, for example, by far the main supplier to rural operators through the 1930s and 1940s, did not offer a diesel engine in its bus chassis until 1953.

This is believed to have been the very first motor bus in Gloucestershire. As with many others of its time, it was little more than an over-grown car. Daimler AD 301 was registered to Mr Edward Silvey of Epney in May 1904 and was put to work on a service between Saul, Epney and Gloucester. Although Daimler was very much a British company, its name came from a German engineer, Gottlieb Daimler, from whom the UK company had bought the British manufacturing rights. This vehicle must have represented a major investment for Mr Silvey; it seems that no expense was spared – note, for example, the elaborate slip board outlining the route. Little is known about the service and there is no record of it having been granted a licence by Gloucester City Council. This may however have arisen through the terminus having been on private property, most likely the yard of a city-centre inn. Licences at that time were only required for vehicles picking up on public thoroughfares, although in later years it was the route itself which required formal authorisation, rather than just the stopping places. The photograph was taken outside the Anchor Inn at Epney. Just to the front of the bus, holding his young daughter Phyllis, is Mr Thomas Stephens, the publican. Note, incidentally, that everyone is wearing some form of headgear. For such a group to be assembled, it may be assumed that this was a special event; it was possibly the vehicle's first day in service. It seems however that the service was short-lived, the vehicle passing to an owner in Brookthorpe for use as a lorry in January 1905. Some years later, other members of the Silvey family were to feature prominently in the provision of bus and coach services in the Epney area (see page seventy-nine).

In the years up to 1921 registration numbers were routinely re-issued in much the same way as 'cherished marks' are today. The number from the Silvey vehicle, AD 301, appeared again in 1914, coincidentally gracing another Daimler. This vehicle was owned by the Dean Forest Contracting Company of Soudley who had acquired it as a car and converted it to a fourteen-seat wagonette. It was put to use on a service from Soudley to Cinderford, running on Friday evenings and on Saturdays. It is probably the vehicle in this view, as the description in the Motor Taxation records is a perfect match with that shown in this advertising postcard. The company was run by the Joiner family and as its name implied, their main occupation was in more general contracting work. While undertaking such work in Stratford-on-Avon in 1927, Mr Stanley Joiner, son of James who was the lead player in the Forest business, made contacts which led to his becoming a co-founder of the Stratford Blue bus company. Stratford Blue quickly became a very successful and much respected operation and was eventually purchased by the Midland Red company; Mr Joiner sold his Stratford interests in 1931 to concentrate on his other activities. The coaching element of Joiner's business appears not to have progressed beyond this wagonette, but Stanley Joiner is believed to have been the main backer of his cousin, C.H. Lewis of Redmarley, who set up a small coach operation in the 1920s, under the trading name of Malvern Green (note the similarity of styling to Stratford Blue!). A number of services were acquired in 1930, connecting villages around Redmarley and Staunton with Malvern, Cheltenham and Gloucester. A number of tours licences was also obtained, although the fleet is thought to have never numbered more than half a dozen vehicles. The business, including the services, was purchased by Bristol Tramways in 1935.

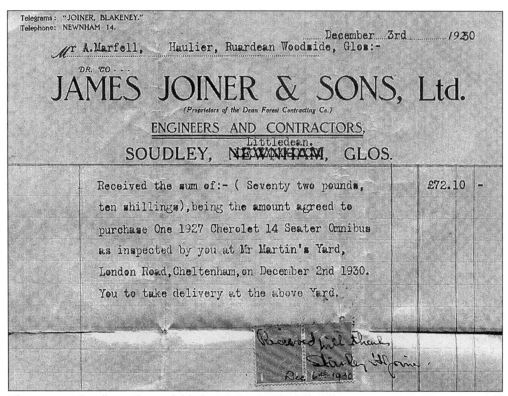

Telegrams: "JOINER, BLAKENEY."
Telephone: NEWNHAM 14.

December 3rd 1930

Mr A.Marfell, Haulier, Ruardean Woodside, Glos:-

DR. TO . . .

JAMES JOINER & SONS, Ltd.

(Proprietors of the Dean Forest Contracting Co.)

ENGINEERS AND CONTRACTORS,

Littledean.

SOUDLEY, NEWNHAM, GLOS.

Received the sum of:- (Seventy two pounds, ten shillings),being the amount agreed to purchase One 1927 Cherolet 14 Seater Omnibus as inspected by you at Mr Martin's Yard, London Road,Cheltenham,on December 2nd 1930. You to take delivery at the above Yard.	£72.10 -

This invoice, kindly made available by Mr Roger Marfell, tells an interesting story. As noted opposite, the Joiner family owned the Dean Forest Contracting Company, but Mr Stanley Joiner at one time also had an interest in the Stratford Blue bus company. This invoice, receipted by Mr Stanley Joiner's signature across the two 1d stamps, covers the sale to Mr A. Marfell (of Marfell Bros) of a 1927 Chevrolet fourteen-seater bus. The bus had been inspected in Mr Martin's yard in Cheltenham. Mr Frank Martin had been granted a taxi licence by Cheltenham Corporation in 1917 and in 1921 bought his first charabanc. In July 1924 he received the Corporation's blessing to run a regular bus service between Cheltenham and Evesham and in 1929 two services between Cheltenham and Malvern were introduced, following different routes. The Stratford Blue company made several applications in 1929 and 1930 to extend its Stratford-on-Avon-Evesham service to Cheltenham, but the Corporation consistently refused to issue a licence in view of the potential abstraction of passengers from Martin's established service. In order to secure the much coveted licences, Stratford Blue eventually persuaded Mr Martin to sell them his operation, concluding the deal in November 1930. As the Malvern services did not fit logically with the Stratford Blue portfolio, they were transferred to the Lewis operation, as mentioned earlier. Rationalisation following the takeover resulted in the sale of several of the eight buses then in the Martin fleet, including this Chevrolet – for £72.10s.

C. H. LEWIS, LTD., Soudley, Littledean, Glos.
TIME TABLES.

Gloucester = Staunton = Malvern.
Via Malvern Wells
WEEKDAYS ONLY.

	a.m.	p.m.	p.m.	S.O. p.m.	S.O. p.m.
Gloucester dep. (Lower Westgate Street)	10 0	3 0	6 0	8 15	9 15
Maisemore ,,	10 6	3 5	6 6	8 21	9 21
Hartpury ,,	1015	3 10	6 15	8 31	9 31
Cross Hands ,,	1020	3 15	6 20	8 35	9 35
Staunton ,,	1025	3 20	6 25	8 40	9 40
Redmarley Chapel ,,	1035	3 25	6 35	......	......
Pendock Cross ,,	1043	3 30	6 43	......	......
Rye Cross ,,	1047	3 35	6 47	......	......
Portsmorton ,,	1050	3 38	6 50	......	......
Castlemorton ,,	1055	3 43	6 55	......	......
Welland ,,	11 0	3 48	7 0	......	......
Hanley Swan ,,	1110	3 55	7 10	......	......
Gt. Malvern arr. (Link Top)	1125	4 10	7 25	......	......

				S.O.	S.O.
Gt. Malvern dep. (Link Top)		1215	4 15	......	7 30
Hanley Swan ,,		1230	4 30	......	7 45
Welland ,,		1240	4 40	......	7 55
Castlemorton ,,		1245	4 45	......	8 0
Rye Cross ,,		1250	4 50	......	8 5
Portsmorton ,,		1253	4 53	......	8 8
Pendock Cross ,,	8 50	1257	4 57	......	8 12
Redmarley Chapel ,,	9 0	1 5	5 5	......	8 20
Staunton ,,	9 10	1 15	5 15	7 15	8 30
Cross Hands ,,	9 20	1 20	5 20	7 20	8 35
Hartpury ,,	9 25	1 25	5 25	7 25	8 40
Maisemore ,,	9 35	1 35	5 35	7 35	8 50
Gloucester arr. (Lower Westgate Street)	9 40	1 40	5 40	7 40	8 55

S.O.—Saturdays only.

Gloucester - Staunton - Upton-on-Severn
MONDAYS, WEDNESDAYS, FRIDAYS & SATURDAYS ONLY.

	a.m.	a.m.	p.m.	p.m	p.m.	S.O. p.m.	S.O. p.m.
Gloucester dep. (Lower Westgate Street)		10 0	......	3 0	6 0	8 15	9 15
Maisemore ,,		10 6	......	3 6	6 6	8 21	9 21
Hartpury ,,		10 15	......	3 15	6 15	8 31	9 31
Corse ,,		10 20	C	3 20	6 20	8 35	9 35
Staunton ,,	8 5	10 25	12 0	3 25	6 25	8 40	9 40
Corse Lawn ,,	8 15	......	12 10	3 36	6 35	......	9 45
Longreen ,,	8 20	......	12 15	3 41	6 40	......	9 50
Longdon ,,	8 27	......	12 22	3 48	......	......	......
Upton-on-Severn arr.	8 37	......	12 32	3 58	......	......	......

C.—Waits for and connects with Bristol Blue Bus leaving Gloucester at 11-30 a.m.

	a.m.	a.m.	p.m.	p.m	p.m.
Upton-on-Severn dep.	8 45	......	12 45	4 45	......
Longdon ,,	8 55	......	12 55	4 55	......
Longreen ,,	9 2	S.O.	1 2	5 2	S.O.
Corse Lawn ,,	9 7	10 10	1 7	5 7	7 10
Staunton ,,	9 10	10 20	1 15	5 15	7 15
Corse ,,	9 20	10 25	1 20	5 20	7 20
Hartpury ,,	9 25	10 30	1 25	5 25	7 25
Maisemore ,,	9 35	10 40	1 35	5 35	7 35
Gloucester arr. (Lower Westgate Street)	9 40	10 45	1 40	5 40	7 40

S.O.—Sarurdays only.

For further particulars apply C. H. Lewis, Ltd., Soudley, Littledean, Glos.   Phone : Newnham 14.   S. H. JOINER, Secretary.

Rec⁴
15 - 3 - 1934

WHEELER, PRINTER, NEWNHAM, GLOS.

The relationship between the bus services of C.H. Lewis and the Joiner family has been outlined on the previous two pages. This 1934 timetable details two of the services from Gloucester through Staunton. Although the Lewis operation was centred on Redmarley, the registered office was at the Joiner base in Soudley, some fifteen miles distant.

Another early Daimler charabanc in the Forest was that belonging to Mr Hancock, licensee of the Bell Inn at Littledean; it was the regular transport for the local football team, but is seen here well-laden with a party setting out from Littledean for the annual Barton Fair in Gloucester around 1919. Although the photograph is somewhat faded, it nevertheless gives a good impression of the tiered seating arrangement in these early vehicles, and the rather cramped conditions which people were only too happy to tolerate for, in many cases, a rare opportunity to venture out of their villages. The Daimler's registration, LX 5649, suggests that it originated from the London area. The Daimler was replaced by a Ford Model T charabanc. Two Vulcans were owned by Mr Hancock during the 1920s but are thought to have been used only as goods vehicles; one however, DD 1282, later served with Walkley of Cinderford and subsequently Gloucestershire Transport as a charabanc.

A more substantial Daimler was this 1914 vehicle which Frank Martin of Cheltenham had fitted out as a thirty-two-seater charabanc. It was registered as AD 9725 when Mr Martin took ¹ᵈ¹ivery of the vehicle in 1921. It is likely that the chassis had previously been fitted with a for use by the War Department. The Daimler was photographed while visiting gh with a party from Cheltenham.

G.J. Miller of Cirencester was running charabancs in the early 1920s and introduced a daily service to Oxford in that same decade, offering connections to London and the coastal areas of the South East. Two new coaches were bought for this service, an ADC and a Leyland Tiger TS2. The weekday services left Cirencester at 8.45a.m. and 3.15p.m., with a Sunday service at 1.30p.m. The day return fare to London, giving just three hours in the capital when this leaflet was issued in 1934, was thirteen shillings.

A very early motor bus operator in the county was Frank Arnold of Nailsworth who had an office in Market Street. The vehicles were garaged at premises in the town's Cossack Square. This Thornycroft 24hp, registered AD 1680, was the first bus in the fleet, having been purchased in October 1910 to operate the three mile service between Nailsworth and Avening. It is seen above at The Cross, its terminus in Avening. The same Thornycroft is seen below on its way from Avening to its home town. In the view above the vehicle looks fairly robust and the road surface appears to be well metalled. In the 'full frontal' view below, the vehicle appears rather less substantial in its construction, and we can see what the road surfaces really could be like on rural stretches; in fact the vehicle received a new body when only a few years old. Thornycroft had experimented with steam vehicle production, but by the early years of the twentieth century was producing petrol-engined vehicles from its new factory at Basingstoke in Hampshire.

The valley through which the Nailsworth-Avening service operated was sparsely populated, and it would seem likely that on any one journey only a few stops would have been made between the two towns. The operation appears to have been a commercial success nonetheless, as Mr Arnold made a significant investment in new vehicles in 1910/11; the Thornycroft being quickly joined by two new taxis, a Charron and a Clement-Bayard, and this Ryknield double-decker. A year or so later, Mr Arnold went on to introduce a motor bus service between Nailsworth and Stroud as the replacement for a horse bus operation run by a Mr Davis. The route followed the main road through Woodchester. This Ryknield became the regular performer on the service. Ryknields were produced in Burton-on-Trent, but the company did not survive long; although they were recognized as quality vehicles, it seems that their potential customers were not prepared to pay a premium for quality products. AD 1786 was sold in 1919 to Cuthbert Moss of Tirley, who ran a bus service from there to Cheltenham; it seems likely that the vehicle would have by then become a single decker, the conversion possibly having been achieved by some fairly basic surgery. A year later it was operating as a lorry for a Cheltenham company. It was replaced in the Arnold fleet by a Scottish-built Caledon double-decker. Although the shadows indicate that the photograph was taken on a sunny day, the crew are well wrapped up. The driver, Mr W. Close, would undoubtedly have needed plenty of warm and water-proof clothing as the vehicle offered him little in the way of protection or comfort. His conductor was Mr Frank Cleaveley. The Arnold business was taken over by the National Omnibus company in 1920.

Messrs Guy Chew and Percy Woolley had formed the Mitcheldean Transport Company early in the twentieth century and later acquired two Straker Squire omnibuses. These are seen at the extreme left of this view of the company's fleet. Next to these vehicles is a pair of Pierce Arrow lorries; that nearest the camera is AD 6875, dating from 1920. This vehicle had been granted a licence to operate a bus service into Gloucester, presumably as a lorry bus. This photograph gives a good impression of the mixed fleets with which road transport pioneers were generally associated.

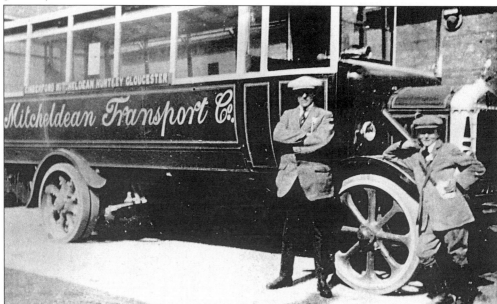

This print provides a better view of one of Mitcheldean Transport's Straker Squires. AD 7857 was also new in 1920 and seated forty passengers – a large vehicle for its time. It was the regular performer on the service from Cinderford to Gloucester via Mitcheldean and Huntley until it caught fire in 1923. The service was then taken over by Bristol Tramways. The other Straker Squire is believed to have been registered L 2904, indicating that it was first registered in Glamorgan, but its history is not known. Straker Squire was at one time a relatively local vehicle builder, operating from Bristol, until relocating to London in around 1920.

The Lydney & Dean Forest Bus Service was a pioneer of local services in the Forest, run by Mr H. T. Letheren. This Daimler Y-type was actually registered AD 8816 but for some strange reason, maybe an error in interpreting its documentation, it masqueraded for most of its life as Y 4571. This was actually its Daimler chassis number! These two views of the

vehicle were both taken in Lydney. Note that the passenger door was only half height. Fresh air was therefore guaranteed – throughout the year! Lydney & Dean Forest was absorbed by Gloucestershire Transport of Lydney in 1926 (part of the Watts empire) and Gloucestershire Transport metamorphosed into Red and White two years later. Mr Letheren continued to run a small coach fleet in Lydney until retiring in 1967; the business was then purchased by Mr James Bevan, and continues to operate from Lydney today.

Mr William Gardner, licensee of the Morning Star at Hardwicke, took delivery of this Hallford fourteen-seater in February 1914. Mr Gardner had originally been a carrier, but in March 1903 introduced a service using a double-decker horse bus from Elmore Lane into Gloucester. In 1904 the bus was joined by a horse-drawn brake. The service remained dependent upon four-legged traction until the Hallford arrived. Its route was captured in the signwriting along the sides of the canopy – Gloucester to Quedgeley, Hardwicke, Moreton (Valence) and Whitminster. The Gloucester terminus was outside Walwin's the chemists, hence the 'where we stop' addition to their advertisement, one of a number which between them have filled the vehicle's body panels. Mr Gardner is seen here standing alongside his vehicle. Curiously the Hallford carried the wrong registration when photographed – it was in fact AD 3610. Hallfords were manufactured in Kent, but vehicle production ceased in the 1920s. From the age of ten, Mr Gardner's daughter Ivy had been a part-time conductress on the vehicles, covering late afternoon and weekend journeys to Gloucester. She was later assisted by her younger brother, George. William Gardner had himself worked in the timber yards in Gloucester, while his wife took care of the public house during the working day. In the evenings Mr Gardner took over in the bar. Despite his obvious energy and business acumen there were few minutes available to him each week for taking any close involvement in his bus operation; this was therefore left in the hands of the drivers, and Mr Gardner's young family. However, the operation was run very successfully, with the vehicles always well turned out, as these photographs reveal. I am very grateful to Mrs Joiner for having made these photographs available for this publication. One or two had suffered a little over the past seventy-plus years – they had for some time been on the walls of the bar in the Morning Star!

Two Caledon E models joined the Gardner fleet, one in each of 1919 and 1920; they are variously described as twenty-nine and thirty-four seaters. They were registered FH 1370 and FH 1888 and their rooftop signboards indicate that the route had been extended beyond Whitminster to Frampton (-on-Severn) and Saul. These two views depict FH 1888. It is seen above negotiating a heavily flooded Bristol Road in Gloucester, and had just passed the Bristol Hotel. Note the bicycle on the roof mounted luggage rack – presumably its owner had decided that the weather was too inclement for him to be able to cycle home! The view below was taken in more favourable conditions. Caledons were built in Scotland, albeit not in any great quantity; they nevertheless enjoyed a ten year production run. (Upper photo: *Gloucester Citizen*)

FH 1370 is seen above in its original form, standing in College Green, Gloucester. When only two years old, this Caledon was rebodied as a charabanc and is seen in that later form below, outside the Bell Inn at Frampton-on-Severn. The Bell stands at the end of the village green, reputed to be the longest such green in the country. Mr William Gardner is seen at the front of the vehicle, with Mr George Nash leaning on the front wing. Mr Nash's son Martin occupies the front seat of the charabanc.

Although the photograph is a little damaged, this view nevertheless shows quite clearly how rapidly coach design advanced during the 1920s, when compared with the 1921 charabanc body on the Caledon on the previous page. This 1928 'all-weather' coach was built by Hall-Lewis on a Thornycroft A6 chassis. The vehicle, also in the Gardner fleet, was registered DF 4777; rather surprisingly it lasted only until 1934. Although well equipped for longer distance travel, and undoubtedly the preferred vehicle for private hire or tours duties, the slip board on the vehicle's side panels indicates that it was required to take its turn on the Gloucester–Frampton service. The young lady in the photograph is probably the late Mrs Ivy Joiner, who provided much information for these captions.

In June 1930 Gardners took delivery of this Albion Viking PKA26 with twenty-six-seat body, probably built locally by Healey. It was the regular on the Gloucester–Frampton service until Bristol Tramways bought the Gardner operation late in 1935; this Albion and a Bedford coach were included in the deal. The Albion was sold by Bristol in 1936 and became a showman's vehicle, working fairgrounds until the early 1950s. It was photographed while fulfilling its final role. Some side windows are panelled over, but the vehicle had undergone very little external modification, and was still very tidy.

From the rudimentary lorry bus depicted in Chapter 3, the Huxley operation was upgraded in about 1930 when this Charron arrived. In the view above Mr Huxley is seen alongside his new vehicle outside the George Inn. In the view below, the vehicle is seen negotiating a flooded stretch of road in its home village. Just visible in the windscreen is the reversible destination board, with South Cerney showing as it heads for home. The vehicle is thought to have been registered E 7107, indicating that it originated in Staffordshire.

Many of the vehicles entering service in the early 1920s were based on surplus War Department chassis, like FH 2684, a 1918 Thornycroft J-type. It is seen here with its new twenty-eight-seat charabanc body standing ready to depart on an outing from Ye Olde Robin Hood Inn in Hopewell Street, Gloucester. Landlord 'Pop' Fletcher is seen in the white hat leaning against the driver's door, while the young lad on the right was Arthur Wood, who coincidentally was the final licensee when the pub closed its door for the last time in the 1970s. The vehicle had been acquired and fitted with its charabanc body in 1922 by Messrs Hough & Whitmore of Gloucester, who went on to become prominent car and truck retailers and for many years held the Vauxhall/Bedford franchise. Visible behind is another Thornycroft J-type, also ex-WD and in this case new in 1915. This one belonged to Davis & Sons of Gloucester and can be seen carrying their 'Westgate' trading name. It was allocated registration AD 8238 when it assumed its civilian role in 1921.

Hough & Whitmore are thought not to have owned any further passenger vehicles, but Davis & Son built up a small fleet. They had commenced the operation of rural services in 1920, when a service from Ross-on-Wye to Gloucester via Ledbury was introduced, closely followed by another Ledbury–Gloucester service, this time via Staunton. The services were purchased by Bristol Tramways in 1931 and the Davis operation then folded. No fewer than five Davis brothers had worked with their father and mother to make the business a success. Looking so much more modern than the Thornycroft in the previous view, FH 4762 was a Dennis three-ton chassis which entered service in April 1927. Its body was by Gloucester Railway & Carriage Company and provided comfortable seating for twenty-six passengers. Pneumatic tyres were by then the norm. Mr Harold Davis is at the wheel as staff of the Gloucester Picturedrome in Barton Street set off on their annual outing. In 1926 one of the Davis brothers, Mr W.H. Davis, broke away from the family firm to set up his own coach business in Gloucester; he later formed a limited company under the name of Glider Pullman Services Ltd. Following two years of success with his first vehicle, two more arrived in 1928 and Glider Pullman obtained a licence for six vehicles to operate a service from Gloucester to Birmingham via Tewkesbury and Worcester, with a extension southward to Bristol added soon afterwards. Although these services were introduced it seems that the additional vehicle licences were not taken up, the pre-existing three vehicles presumably covering the work adequately. However, all was not well and a receiver was appointed towards the end of 1929, Midland Red taking over operation of the service to Birmingham.

BETTER & CHEAPER BY ROAD

GLIDER PULLMAN SERVICES.
REGULAR DAILY SERVICE BETWEEN

BIRMINGHAM

Worcester, Tewkesbury, Gloucester and

BRISTOL

Depart BIRMINGHAM—9 a.m. to BRISTOL.
(Dale End Coach Station.)

,, B'HAM to GLOUCESTER—9 a.m. 12-15 3-30 6-30 p.m.

,, BRISTOL—10-30 a.m., 2 p.m., 5 p.m.

FARES.		Single	Return
BIRMINGHAM to BRISTOL		7/-	12/6
,, ,, GLOUCESTER		4/6	7/-
,, ,, TEWKESBURY		4/6	6/6
,, ,, Upton-on-Severn		3/-	5/6
,, ,, WORCESTER		2/3	4/-

RETURN TICKETS AVAILABLE FOR ONE MONTH.
Children under 3 years, free, over 3 and under 12, half fare.

WHERE TO BOOK:
The HOLIDAY ACCOMMODATION BUREAU, 9, Dale End,
Birmingham. Tel. Central 214.

PARK GARAGES (Aston) Ltd., Lichfield Rd. Nr. Salford Bridge. East 312.
Messrs HASTILOW'S 8 Parade, Sutton Coldfield. Tel. S. Coldfield 238.
,, BRUCE Tobacconist, 1100 Warwick Rd., Acocks Green. A. Green 400
Miss. E. WEBB, Ladies' Outfitter, 311, Victoria Rd., Aston.
DALTON'S GARAGE, Soho Road, Handsworth. North. 457.
H. HIGGINBOTHAM, 359, Bearwood Road, Smethwick. Bearwood 1273.
HUDSON'S MUSIC STORE, Lower Union Street, Bristol.
MUNN, Newsagent, Upton-on-Severn.
HOPKINS, Tobacconist, The Cross, Tewkesbury.
CARTER, Stationer, Northgate Street, Gloucester.
PERKS TRAVEL BOOKINGS, Southgate Street, Gloucester.

CONDITIONS OF TRAVEL.

All Seats must be booked in advance. No responsibility can
be accepted if passengers are not at the point specified at the time stated for
starting.

Hand Luggage only not exceeding 26"×15"×7" will be carried free at owners' risk.
(Suitcases may be hired at small charge.)

This handbill set out details of the short-lived Glider Pullman operations between Birmingham and Bristol.

Another vehicle which used to operate into Gloucester was this Ford TT, registered DD 475. The vehicle was new in March 1922 to Mr Arthur Freeman, licensee of the Queens' Arms at Ashleworth. In 1923 Gloucester City Council granted him a licence to run a service into the City. It was not Mr Freeman's first bus – he had previously operated a thirteen-seat Simplex wagonette – but the Ford was undoubtedly a big improvement! The Ford later passed to Messrs Turley and Bennett of Blakeney but had completed its days as a passenger vehicle by 1931. It was eventually rescued and restored by Mr Melville Watts of Lydney and is seen on display at a vintage vehicle rally in Cardiff Civic Centre in 1977. The vehicle is left-hand drive, a feature of many Model Ts. Note that passenger access was in this case via the rear of the vehicle. Mr Watts is the son of Mr Arthur Watts who, with his brother John, transformed the family's modest business in Lydney into what became the Watts Group of Companies, which continues to thrive today. Arthur's particular success, combining his business and engineering talents, lay in the repatriation of many lorries, surplus to the requirements of the War Department, following the end of the Great War, and their subsequent refurbishment and sale. His brother concentrated on the development of transport operations, primarily bus services in the Forest of Dean and South Wales, laying the foundation for what was soon to become the Red and White group of companies.

AYLAND'S BUS SERVICES.

June 1930

Westbury to Gloucester via Rodley.

MONDAY, WEDNESDAY, FRIDAY

		a.m.	a.m.	p.m.	p.m.
WESTBURY ...	depart	9 30	11 30	2 30	4 30
RODLEY	,,	9 40	11 40	2 40	4 40
CHAXHILL ...	,,	9 50	11 50	2 50	4 50
MINSTERWORTH	,,	10 0	12 0	3 0	5 0
GLOUCESTER	arrive	10 15	12 15	3 15	5 15
GLOUCESTER	depart	10 45	12 45	3 45	5 45
MINSTERWORTH	,,	11 0	1 0	4 0	6 0
CHAXHILL ...	,,	11 10	1 10	4 10	6 10
RODLEY	,,	11 20	1 20	4 20	6 20
WESTBURY ...	arrive	11 30	1 30	4 30	6 30

SATURDAY.

		a.m.	a.m.	p.m.	p.m.	p.m.
WESTBURY ...	depart	9 0	10 30	2 30	6 30	8 30
RODLEY	,,	9 10	10 40	2 40	6 40	8 40
CHAXHILL ...	,,	9 20	10 50	2 50	6 50	8 50
MINSTERWORTH	,,	9 30	11 0	3 0	7 0	9 0
GLOUCESTER	arrive	9 45	11 15	3 15	7 15	9 15
GLOUCESTER	depart	9 45	12 45	3 45	7 45	11 0
MINSTERWORTH	,,	10 0	1 0	4 0	8 0	11 15
CHAXHILL ...	,,	10 10	1 10	4 10	8 10	11 25
RODLEY	,,	10 20	1 20	4 20	8 20	11 35
WESTBURY ...	arrive	10 30	1 30	4 30	8 30	11 45

SUNDAY.

		p.m.	p.m.	p.m.
WESTBURY ...	depart	2 0	6 0	9 0
RODLEY	,,	2 10	6 10	9 10
CHAXHILL ...	,,	2 20	6 20	9 20
MINSTERWORTH	,,	2 30	6 30	9 30
GLOUCESTER	arrive	2 45	6 45	9 45
GLOUCESTER	depart	2 45	6 45	10 0
MINSTERWORTH	,,	3 0	7 0	10 15
CHAXHILL ...	,,	3 10	7 10	10 25
RODLEY	,,	3 20	7 20	10 35
WESTBURY ...	arrive	3 30	7 30	10 45

Fares :

Westbury to Rodley	..	**3d.**	Westbury to Chaxhill	..	**5d.**
Westbury to Minsterworth		**6d.**	Westbury to Gloucester		**10d.**

Also an early operator of motor buses along the north bank of the Severn was Mr Alfred Ayland of Westbury-on-Severn. In 1921 he was granted a licence by Gloucester Corporation to operate a Ford Model T on a service from Westbury into the City. The Ayland business continued until Alfred's son (also Alfred) sold out to Soudley Valley Coaches in 1953, although he continued to drive for that concern for some years afterwards. This was the 1930s timetable for the Westbury service.

George Pritchett started in business with a horse-drawn carrier's van working into Cirencester from the villages around Bibury. One of his nine sons, Fred, took over the business in the 1920s. The first motor vehicle to be acquired was this most unusual Dearborn FX. Dearborn was a US manufacturer who exported small numbers of chassis to the UK, most of which received goods bodies. DD 1770 arrived with Pritchetts in January 1923 and remained until 1931. It was subsequently rescued for preservation and was photographed at a vintage show in the 1970s. The body was built by Constable and seated fourteen. Pritchetts only ever owned four buses, one at a time, and ceased operations in 1958. Not only is this Dearborn in preservation but so is Pritchett's horse-drawn cart. The latter has been on display in the Bristol Industrial Museum for some years.

TIME TABLE.

BIBURY, BARNSLEY, CIRENCESTER.

Place.	Mondays.		Tues:	Wednesdays.			Thrs:	Fridays.			Saturdays.
	a.m	p.m.	p.m.	a.m.	p.m.	p.m.	a.m.	a.m.	p.m.	p.m.	p.m.
Bibury, Sqr: Dept:	10-0	1-20	1-20	10-0	1-20	5-20	10-0	10-0	1-20	1-20	5-20
Barnsley	10-15	1-35	1-35	10-15	1-35	5-35	10-15	10-15	1-35	1-35	5-35
Cirencester, Arr:	10-30	1-50	1-50	10-30	1-50	5-50	10-30	10-30	1-50	1-50	5-50
Cirencester, Dept:	12-0 N	4-0	4-0	12-0	4-0	8-15	12-0	12-0	4-0	4-0	8-30

The above Services are in Operation MAY / SEPTEMBER.

PRITCHETT & SON.

When issued in April 1936, two of Pritchett's Wednesday journeys had been deleted from this time-table – it seems probable that they were only provided during the summer months.

A rather more solid-looking vehicle than many of its generation was this 1923 Vulcan VSD, one of two to be delivered to Daniel Walkley of Cinderford in July of that year. The smartly attired driver looks suitably proud of his vehicle which was probably newly delivered when the photograph was taken. Vulcan themselves were also seemingly proud of this vehicle, registered DD 3042; not only does their name appear in the customary position at the top of the radiator, but also on the bonnet sides and at the base of each of the four side windows! Walkleys had been in transport since the late nineteenth century when brothers Aaron and Moses Walkley introduced a regular horse-drawn service from their home at Ruspidge into Gloucester. Their sons Daniel and Joseph took over at around the turn of the century, and motorisation eventually followed, the earliest known vehicles, a Pagefield and a Minerva, both arriving in 1919. No fewer than nine Vulcan buses were purchased in the 1920s. The operation was taken over by Gloucestershire Transport (later Red and White) in 1926, but Walkleys returned to small-scale coach operation shortly afterwards, continuing into the 1930s.

Mr Albert Meek's lorry bus was illustrated in Chapter 3; his next Ford Model T was fitted with a conventional bus body. DF 665 was supplied new in August 1926 with a fourteen-seat body, built by Allen. This was to be the regular performer on Meek's service between Ruardean and Cinderford via The Morse for several years. It is seen here at Cinderford, in The Triangle. Note that vehicles receiving saloon bodies had by this time received all-round glazing, thus making life for the driver and his passengers much more comfortable. Standing alongside are conductor Ron Hatch and Mr Albert Meek himself (by the front wheel). In these days when we are accustomed to double-decker buses, seating in some cases more than eighty, and operated only by the driver, the concept of a conductor attending to the needs of no more than fourteen passengers seems a little curious. Mr Meek sold the bus business, then comprising three coaches, to Edwards of Joy's Green in 1955.

Meek's never had a vehicle quite as grand as that illustrated in the letterhead they were using in the 1940s!

36, Worcester Street, Gloucester.

Messrs. A. Meek & Son,   18/8/   1926.

Nailbridge, Glos.

Dr. to P. V. TAYLOR & CO.

AUTHORISED *Ford* DEALERS.
THE UNIVERSAL CAR

1926.	R549.			
18/8.	To "Ford" One Ton Chassis, low speed, heavy cords, completely equipped as per manufacturers specification.			
	Chassis No. 13791769. Reg No. DF665.			
	Fitted with 14 Seater "Allen" Saloon Bus.			
	"Supaphord" 4 speed Gear Box fitted.			
	Dynamo Lighting fitted.			
	2 Interior Lights fitted.			
	No. Plates & Licence Holder.			
	Delivery Charges.		£325.0.0	
	Extras.			
	Lettering. £1. 15. 0.			
	Dome front wings. 1. 15. 0.			
	Step at rear. 17. 6.			
	Tax. 4. 8. 0.		8.15.6.	
			£333.15.6.	
	Less Deposit £25. 0. 0.			
	Allowance for Bus. 90. 0. 0.		£115. 0.0.	
			£218.15.6.	
			1 10 0	
			£217 5 6	

Today a fourteen-seat minibus might be expected to cost around £30,000 – and a top of the range fifty-seat touring coach some seven times that amount. In 1926 Meek's DF 665 illustrated on the previous page cost just £333. This is the original invoice showing that the vehicle was supplied by P.V. Taylor of Gloucester, who were the City's Ford agent for very many years.

Another Ford fourteen-seater for Meek's Cinderford-Ruardean service was DF 7458. This April 1929 delivery was an AA model. Alongside is driver Horace Hook. The photograph was taken at the Nailbridge depot, at the junction of the Drybrook, Ruardean and Cinderford roads.

This viewcard is a tranquil view of a rural bus laying over in a Forest town. The town is Ruardean and the bus is one of Meek's Ford AAs, probably DF 7458 again. It waits in The Square for its next trip. The picture is dated 19 August 1938; the long shadows indicate late afternoon. But where is everyone? A young lad watches the photographer, a mother trundles a push chair along the street and there is a bicycle propped outside the shop. With the bus is driver Bert Smith, enjoying a cigarette in the summer sunshine. The shop in the right foreground displays an agency sign for the 'Gloster Red and White' parcels service. During the transition from Gloucestershire Transport to Red and White in 1928, the trading name of Gloster Red and White was used.

FORM P.S.V. 2/H

LICENCE No. H00,504

PLATE No. H 500.

ROAD TRAFFIC ACT, 1930.
PUBLIC SERVICE VEHICLE LICENCE.

We, the TRAFFIC COMMISSIONERS for the **WESTERN** TRAFFIC AREA, hereby license—

Name......Meek & Co.,

Address............Hill View,

.....................Nailbridge, Nr. Drybrook, Glos.......

(First change—see Note 3) ....

....

to use the motor vehicle described below as a .....stage.............. carriage in accordance with the provisions of the Road Traffic Act, 1930.

This licence shall have effect as from the .4th June............. 1931. and shall continue in force for one year from that date.

DESCRIPTION OF VEHICLE.

Index mark and registration number (see Note 1 overleaf)...D.F.7458...........

Make, model and year of manufacture of chassis.....................................
.....Ford 1929.........................,.............

Chassis Number..1012238...... Seating Capacity, Lower deck.....14...........
Upper deck.....................

General description :—

(i) Four wheeled or six wheeled.................Four.............................
(ii) Pneumatic tyred or otherwise...............Pneumatic.....................
(iii) Single or double decked........................Single............................
(iv) Type of body.....................................Saloon...........................

....

And we hereby acknowledge the receipt of the sum of £3 (three pounds) being the fee payable on the grant of this licence.

Dated this..........4th.............. day of..... June............193.1.

F. Nicholson

For and on behalf of the

TRAFFIC COMMISSIONERS FOR THE   **WESTERN**   TRAFFIC AREA.

[OVER

Under the Road Traffic Act of 1930, any vehicle falling within the newly-introduced Public Service Vehicle (PSV) regulations needed an individual licence, to be granted by the Traffic Commissioners of the area concerned. Gloucestershire fell within the Western area based in Bristol and it was from there that this licence was issued for Albert Meek's Ford, DF 7458, for the twelve month period commencing 4 June 1931. PSVs thereafter were no longer required to display the large Hackney plates, small licence discs being introduced for display in their front screens.

DG 6293 was also a fourteen-seat Ford AA, but looked rather different as its body had been constructed to coach specifications by Jenkins of Harvington. It was purchased new by Albert Meek in April 1933. The destination is set at Cinderford, indicating that this coach worked alongside its bus-bodied stable-mates maintaining the local service.

Contrasting with their lorry bus in Chapter 3, one of Marfell Bros' later vehicles was this 1931 Chevrolet. It was to be one of the last Chevrolets delivered new in the area, the first Bedfords appearing just a few months later. DG 1847 is seen outside its garage in Ruardean Woodside. The garage still stands and the premises today continue to provide the base for the Marfell family's transport operations. In addition to miners' services to Waterloo and Cannop collieries, Marfells also provided a public service from Ruardean to Cinderford, and were later granted a licence for operating excursions and tours from Ruardean. The Marfell Bros' fleet was standardised on Chevrolets and Bedfords; the final two Bedfords were sold to Edwards Coaches of Joy's Green in 1943.

Joys Green Bus Service

REVISED TIME TABLE
Commencing May 8th, 1937
JOYS GREEN -- CINDERFORD

	p.m.	p.m		p.m.	p.m.	p.m.
Joys Green ...	3.25	4.25	Every hour until	8 25	10. 0	11. 0
Lydbrook	3.30	4.30		8.30	10. 5	11. 5
Brierley	3.40	4.40		8.40	10.15	11.15
Cinderford	3.55	4.55		8.55	10 25	11.25
					*	*
	p.m.	p.m.		p.m.	p.m.	p.m.
Cinderford	4. 0	5. 0	Every hour until	9. 0	10.30	11.50
Brierley	4.10	5.10		9.10	10.45	12. 5
Lydbrook	4.20	5.20		9.20	10.55	12.15
Joys Green	4.25	5.25		9.25	11. 0	12.20

* To wait termination of Cinema and the Dance at the Welfare Hall

Special Quotations given for Outing Clubs and Parties

Forest of Dean Newspapers, Ltd.

Edwards of Joy's Green was to become the county's largest independent operator in the 1970s with, for a brief period, over forty vehicles on the road. In the pre-war years however the business, which had first appeared in the 1920s, ran just a handful of vehicles. In this 1937 timetable the name Joy's Green Bus Service is used, but this was descriptive only and never in formal use. As their letterhead below reveals the company normally traded under the name of W.T. Edwards & Sons.

W. T. EDWARDS & SONS

Motor Coach Proprietors

JOYS GREEN
LYDBROOK - GLOS.

Telephone No.: LYDBROOK 206

COACHES FOR HIRE

PRIVATE PARTIES A SPECIALITY

Brothers Cecil and Harold Warner first set up in business when they returned home to Twyning after service in the First World War. Warner Bros initially concentrated on supporting the local agricultural community, undertaking ploughing and scuffling and repairing farm equipment. Only a year or two had elapsed before they bought a Ford Model T truck, which was converted for use as a lorry bus. With the Ford they commenced a service from Twyning into Tewkesbury. These are Warner Bros' first premises at Twyning, around 1926. In the doorway are Harold Warner with his son Norman and, in the white smock, Ron Wakeford. Just visible on the original print on the Warner Bros nameboard to the left can be seen '…seater bus and one ton lorry for hire', the Model T fulfilling both of these roles.

Soon after the Ford, a Fiat bus arrived and then in June 1925 came this Thornycroft A1. The vehicle, photographed when new, was registered DD 7399 and seated twenty passengers. It has a very neat body, albeit with a noticeably arched roofline.

A slightly newer Thornycroft quickly followed. RL 2727 was a second-hand purchase, or possibly a diverted order, its registration indicating a Cornish connection. The Twyning arm of the Warner family ceased bus operations in the early 1930s and the Thornycroft was converted for use as a lorry. It was sold on to a farmer in Twyning but was eventually re-acquired by the Warner family who had a replica charabanc body constructed some sixty years after the original had been built. The fully restored vehicle is above seen while on display at the Stroud Show in 1986. Note the Hackney Carriage plate affixed to the rear stating its approved seating capacity. This was a legal requirement at the time, perpetuated today for taxis, for which local authorities continue to hold licensing powers. The Road Traffic Act of 1930 transferred licensing of buses, coaches and the services which they operated to newly-appointed regional Traffic Commissioners. The more conventional frontal view below shows the vehicle waiting to join the 1991 Tewkesbury Carnival parade.

One of the Warner Bros, Cecil, left the Twyning partnership in 1928 and set up a new garage and coach business in Tewkesbury High Street. One of his first vehicles was the fourteen-seat Ford AA in these two views. DG 1123 was bodied in Cheltenham by Tyler and Martin and entered service in September 1930. Tyler and Martin are thought to have constructed bodies for only seven or eight coaches; their main work was the construction of car bodies, some of which were still being built to individual specification in the 1930s. In post-war years Tyler and Martin's main activity was vehicle repair; some such work was the result of mishaps, but replacement or strengthening of timber framing was also regularly required on vehicles at that time.

AJS of Wolverhampton were well known as motorcycle manufacturers, but they did produce small numbers of larger vehicles. The Pilot model was specifically built as a coach chassis. DG 4390 was completed as a twenty-six-seater for Cecil Warner by Tyler and Martin in May 1932. These views were taken at the Tyler and Martin factory in Cheltenham before the vehicle was delivered to Tewkesbury. This is thought to have been the largest vehicle constructed by the Cheltenham coachbuilder.

DG 6683 arrived with Warner's in June 1933. It was a Leyland Cub KP2. The 'K' showed that its chassis was produced at Leyland's plant at Kingston-on-Thames, where most Leyland lighter vehicles were manufactured, while the 'P' defined it as a Passenger model. Duple provided the twenty-seat coach body. The Cub is seen ready to set off from the Abbey Mills in Tewkesbury with a staff outing; this viewcard is dated 5 September 1935. Mr Cecil Warner was himself the driver on this occasion. Annual coach outings were arranged by many organisations in the days before widespread car ownership. For some people they still represented a rare opportunity to get away from their own towns and villages.

Bedford WLB DG 8984 was delivered to Miles Coaches of Guiting Power in 1934. The vehicle had a twenty-seat Duple bus body and was regularly deployed on the daily stage services into Cheltenham. Mr Wilf Miles is seen with the coach soon after delivery.

MILES'
Daily Motor Coach Services.

ROUTE :
Guiting, Hawling, Brockhampton, Andoversford and Cheltenham.

Agreed Time Table Commencing : May 27th

Leaving	Monday a.m. p.m	Tuesday a.m. p.m.	Wednesday a.m. p m.	Thursday a.m. p.m.	Friday a m. p m.	Saturday a.m. p.n.	Sunday p m.
Guiting	9 0 1 25	9 0 1 25	9 0 1 25	9 0 1 25 7 0	9 0 1 25	9 0 1 25 5 30 9 30	1 40 8 45
Hawling	1 40	9 15 1 40	1 40	9 15 1 40 7 15	9 15 1 40	9 15 1 40 5 40	1 55 9 0
Brockhampton	9 25 1 45	9 25 1 45	9 25 1 45	9 25 1 45 7 20	9 25 1 45	9 25 1 45 5 45 9 50	2 p.m 9 5
Sevenhampton	9 30 1 50	9 30 1 50	9 30 1 50	9 30 1 50 7 25	9 30 1,50	9 30 1 50 5 50 9 55	2 5 9 10
Andoversford	9 35 1 55	9 35 1 55	9 35 1 55	9 35 1 55 7 30	9 35 1 55	9 35 1 55 6 0 10 0	2 10 9 15
East End	9 50 2 10	9 50 2 10	9 50 2 10	9 50 2 10 7 45	9 50 2 10	9 50 2 10 6 15 10 15	2 20 9 30
ARRIVE Cheltenham	9 55 2 15	9 55 2 15	9 55 2 15	9 55 2 15 7 50	9 55 2 15	9 55 2 15 6 20 10 25	2 25 9 35
DEPART Cheltenham	12 15 5 45 Not via Hawling	12 15 5 45	12 15 5 45 Not via Hawling	12 15 5 45 8 40	12 15 5 45	12 15 4 30 8 40 10 55	3 10 9 40

ALL SERVICES START AT THE SQUARE LOWER GUITING AND DEPART FROM THE CROWN HOTEL YARD CHELTENHAM-

CAR FOR HIRE, ALSO ONE 20 SEATS PULLMAN SALOON COACH.

For Your Tours and Outings apply to W. G. MILES, Lower Guiting. Any number quoted for any distance.

The vehicle history of Miles Coaches of Guiting Power is typical of so many small rural operations. A horse-drawn carrier's cart was acquired in 1896 and probably continued in use until a Daimler carrier's van was acquired in 1919, almost certainly after military service. The inevitable Ford Model T and Ford AA arrived in the 1920s. Bedfords then found favour, and apart from a Commer operated during the Second World War and a later Morris minibus, held sway until the coach operation was sold in 1968. In this case Pulhams were the purchaser, taking two of the Bedfords into their own fleet, but releasing the oldest vehicle for sale to a local school. Miles retained the village garage at Guiting and continued to operate a minibus until 1980. Pulhams continue to out-park a coach at Guiting to cover Miles' former route into Cheltenham. The raison d'etre for the Miles operation was always the regular service into Cheltenham. This was the timetable in use in the 1930s.

Bicycles were clearly as significant a feature of Oxford's townscape in the 1930s as they are today! Here three frame this 1933 Commer Centaur with twenty-seat coach body by Constable. DG 7862 was representing Harvey's Coaches of Chedworth. Mr Francis Harvey, better known as Ralph, had been running a general garage business at Chedworth in the 1920s; this included several trucks and in around 1928 he acquired his first bus. Services were started from Chedworth to Cheltenham and Cirencester, and although that to Cirencester was sold to Clements of Barnsley in 1933, the service came back into the Harvey fold in 1940 when the Clements business was purchased. The Cheltenham service was sold to Perrett's Coaches in 1970, but Harvey's Coaches continued to trade and run into Cirencester until 1998, despite passing out of the family' ownership in 1972. The Commer in this view enjoyed a long life. In 1940 it passed to Smith of Kemble and then in 1951 moved on to Ayling in the same village for its final year as a PSV.

Another Harvey vehicle was WV 1315. This was a Bedford WLB with twenty-seater coachwork. It was a year older than the Commer and is seen in the heart of the Cotswold countryside.

HARVEY'S
MOTOR 'BUS SERVICE.

DAILY SERVICE BETWEEN
CHEDWORTH, WITHINGTON, KILKENNY. DOWDESWELL. AND CHELTENHAM.

TIME TABLE AS FROM MAY. 1st. 1933

Depart --	MON. TUES. WED.		THURSDAY			FRIDAY		SATURDAY			SUNDAY	
	a.m.	p.m.	a m.	p.m	p.m.	a m.	p m.	a m.	p.m.	p.m,	p.m,	p.m.
Chedworth L. ...	9 45	1 35	9 45	2 5	6 5	9 45	1 35	9 45	2 5	6 5	1 10	8 30
Chedworth, U. ...	9 50	1 40	9 50	2 10	6 10	9 50	1 40	9 50	2 10	6 10	1 15	8 35
Withington ...	10 5	1 55	10 5	2 25	6 25	10 5	1 55	10 5	2 25	6 25	1 30	8 50
Kilkenny ...	10 15	2 5	10 15	2 35	6 35	10 15	2 5	10 15	2 35	6 35	1 40	9 0
Dowdeswell ...	10 17	2 7	10 17	2 37	6 37	10 17	2 7	10 17	2 37	6 37	1 42	9 2
Cheltenham (arrive **ROYAL YARD**.	10 35	2 25	10 35	2 55	6 55	10 35	2 25	10 35	2 55	6 55	1 57	9 20

PLEASE NOTE
NEW DEPARTURE STATION.

Returning from **ROYAL YARD** OPPOSITE CADENA CAFE HIGH STREET.

Depart—	Monday Tuesday Wednesday		Thursday			Friday		Saturday *			Sunday		
	p.m,	p m.	p.m.	p.m.	p m.	p.m.	p.m.	p.m.	p.m	p.m.	p.m,	p.m.	p.m.
Cheltenham **ROYAL YARD**	12 15	5 0	12 15	3 30	9 10	12 15	5 0	12 15	5 0	9 10	10 50	2 45	10 0
Dowdeswell	12 30	5 15	12 30	3 45	9 25	12 30	5 15	12 30	5 15	9 25	11 5	3 0	10 15
Kilkenny	12 32	5 17	12 32	3 47	9 27	12 32	5 17	12 32	5 17	9 27	11 7	3 2	10 17
Withington	12 42	5 27	12 42	3 57	9 37	12 42	5 27	12 42	5 27	9 37	11 17	3 12	10 27
Chedworth, U. ...	12 57	5 42	12 57	4 12	9 52	12 57	5 42	12 57	5 43		11 32	3 27	10 42
Chedworth, L.	1 5	5 50	1 5	4 20	10 0	1 5	5 50	1 5	5 50	*	11 40	3 35	10 50

* TO WITHINGTON ONLY

We shall endeavour to run at the advertised times, but cannot hold ourselves responsible for any delay which may occur. and reserve the right to withdraw or alter any of the above Services.

QUOTATIONS FOR PRIVATE PARTIES, Etc

The Garage, Chedworth 'Phone Foss Bridge 29.

The two Harvey vehicles depicted on the previous page will have been regular performers on the company's main stage service, that from Chedworth to Cheltenham. This timetable was introduced in the summer of 1933.

As noted in Chapter 1, Cottrell's of Mitcheldean began operations as a nineteenth century carrier. Motorization had arrived by 1921 when a Ford Model T wagonette was acquired. This was followed in 1923 by a Garford and an Oldsmobile, both of which seated fourteen, but in very different bodies. The Garford was registered FH 2887 and as may be made out in the view above it had an enclosed bus body. It seems likely that this would have been the regular performer on the service to Gloucester. The vehicle was in use until early 1927. In the picture below is FH 3008, the American-built Oldsmobile. This was fitted with an open charabanc body. The Oldsmobile too was sold before 1930, passing to W.T. Edwards of Joy's Green, and may have been the first bus in what was to become a very large fleet.

The next arrival at Mitcheldean was DF 981, a Chevrolet X with fourteen-seat Willmott body. This vehicle was delivered new in October 1926 and appears to have been a replacement for the Garford. It is seen at the Mitcheldean depot before setting out for Gloucester. This vehicle lasted less than three years with Cottrells and moved across the Severn to join the fleet of Reyne in Stroud.

In June 1927 another Chevrolet arrived at Mitcheldean; DF 2958 also carried a fourteen-seat body by Willmott. It is seen here when newly delivered.

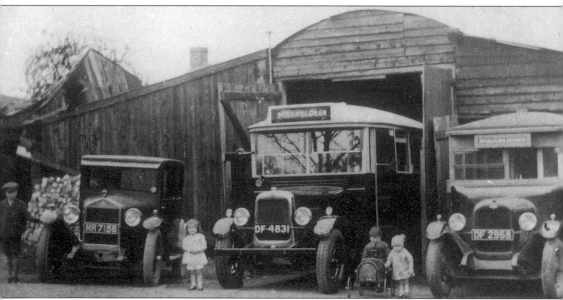

In this view of Cottrells' garage, the 1927 Chevrolet is accompanied by DF 4831, a GMC T20 twenty-seater dating from April 1928. GMC and Chevrolet were both members of the General Motors group. Also shown is Essex Super Six MR 7158, one of several cars in the early fleet. Four of Mr F.C. Cottrell's five children are in this scene. In the pedal car is Bruce Cottrell and with him is his brother Edgar; these two were to take over responsibility for the company following their father's death in 1970. Cottrell's is still held in high regard by other local operators and has entered the twenty-first century with a fleet of thirteen buses and coaches. Edgar Cottrell is in sole control following the death of his brother in 1998. The route of their grandfather's carrier operation had been extended beyond Mitcheldean to Drybrook, with a later extension to Ruardean. This service continues today, providing Ruardean with a two-hour frequency for much of the day. Mitcheldean Transport had introduced a service through the village from which they took their name, en route from Cinderford to Gloucester. The route passed to Bristol Tramways in the 1920s and as part of a package of adjustments following nationalisation of major bus operators in the post-war years, the route passed to Red and White, along with Bristol's other commitments in the Forest area. Following Red and White's retrenchment in the 1970s, Cottrells became responsible for the two-hourly service, returning the operation to the independent sector after a gap of some fifty years. The combined frequency of the Ruardean and Cinderford services on the section between Mitcheldean and the city is hourly during the working week, normally operated by double-deckers and with the Ruardean journeys still crew-operated. I am very grateful to Alan Cottrell, son of Bruce, for the provision of photographs and information.

TELEPHONE: DRYBROOK 224

SUN SALOON COACHES
FOR HIRE

ANY NUMBER CATERED FOR

P.V.O.A.

F. C. COTTRELL

Motor Coach Proprietor

POSTAL ADDRESS

MILL END, MITCHELDEAN, Gloucester

Star Flyer DF 7511 joined the Cottrell fleet in 1929, in effect a replacement for the Oldsmobile – but what a different vehicle it was! A twenty-six-seat all-weather coach body was fitted. Stars were built in Wolverhampton and the company was acquired by its near neighbour, Guy, in 1928. The Star name continued until 1932 when production ceased.

Cottrells purchased three new Dennis's in the early 1930s. A pair of Lancets arrived in 1932/33, each with a Duple thirty-two-seat coach body. One of the Lancets is seen in this view, thought to have been taken at Barry Island, a popular destination for day trips from the Forest area. Although not much of the coach is visible, some distinctive early 1930s features are apparent: curtains at the windows which are themselves of the half-drop variety, sliding rear door, roof-mounted luggage rack and very straight roof and waist-rails. Two of Cottrell's drivers can be seen, indicating that there was probably another representative from the fleet nearby. In uniform at the left is the then proprietor, Mr F.C. Cottrell.

The 1932 Lancet was DG 4736, caught in rather less clement weather, ploughing along a flooded stretch of road through Churcham, on service between Mitcheldean and Gloucester in hot pursuit of an Austin Seven Ruby saloon. The date was January 1936. (Photo: *Gloucester Citizen*)

Duple also bodied this twenty-seat Dennis Ace, which took up residence in Mitcheldean in June 1934. DG 9516 is seen about to pick up a family group for a day out.

BAT was a small Bristol-based venture which produced PSV chassis for just two years before succumbing to the competition of its much larger rivals. The smaller of its two models was the Cruiser and an example was DG 1077, supplied new to Cottrell's of Mitcheldean in September 1930. It was fitted with a twenty-seater body. When only a year old the vehicle passed to Mr Basil Howse of Aldsworth, who used it on his small network of services in the Aldsworth/Cirencester/Cheltenham area. The BAT was photographed while in Howse's ownership, and Mr Howse is seen alongside. Howse's bus operations were bought by Marchant's Coaches of Cheltenham in 1952, although the Howse family continued with a haulage business at Aldsworth for many years thereafter.

HOWSE'S MOTOR SERVICES, ALDSWORTH.

ALDSWORTH and CHELTENHAM.

THURSDAYS		Fares			SATURDAYS	
Depart	p.m.	S.	R.		Depart	p.m.
Aldsworth	1 0	1/6	3/-		Aldsworth	4 0
Barrington	1 20	1/6	3/-		Barrington	4 20
Windrush	1 30	1/6	2/9		Windrush	4 30
Sherborne	1 40	1/3	2/6		Sherborne	4 40
Northleach	1 55	1/3	2/6		Northleach	4 50
Cheltenham arr: 2 30					arr: Cheltenham 5 25	
dep: Plough Yard 6 30. p.m.					dep: Plough Yard 10 30. p.m.	

14 and 20 SEATER SALOON BUSES FOR HIRE.

Estimates on Application   B.G.Howse. Proprietor.

HARVEY CHEDWORTH GLOS

This timetable sets out details of Howse's services between Aldsworth and Cheltenham in the 1930s.

Deciding what was a 'bus' in the years before the 1930 Road Traffic Act is not as easy as it might appear. The dividing line between buses and trucks can be somewhat grey, as Chapter 3 makes clear. Equally the distinction between taxis and small buses is far from obvious. In this postcard of the Triangle at Cinderford, the similarity between the two categories may be seen. Clearly visible, despite damage to the print, is DD 8464, a Ford Model T taxi belonging to Mr Robins of Cinderford, licensed to carry five passengers. In front is a fourteen-seater Morris Commercial T-type bus. It was registered DD 6602 and owned by Kenneth Paulson of High Street, Cinderford. Both vehicles carry Hackney licence plates above their rear registration plates – there was no licensing distinction between taxis and buses in the years before 1931.

Although a rule of thumb is that buses seat eight or more, this 1908 Mors 24hp seven-seater car was used as a bus, to provide a regular service between Cinderford and Gloucester. The Mors was operated by Forest of Dean Road Motors of Parkend, who obtained registration AD3043 when they acquired the vehicle in 1913. Five passengers could sit within the enclosed saloon, while the other two would sit with the driver, with the benefit of full air-conditioning.

Mr Paulson operated several small Morris buses. A year newer than that in the photograph opposite was DD 9383, also a fourteen-seater T-type. Kenneth Paulson ran two services from Cinderford, one to Drybrook and the other to Ross-on-Wye. The operation was bought out by the rapidly expanding Red and White in 1931. Standing in front of the Morris is its smartly-attired driver, Mr Fred Palfrey.

Like its older sister, DD 9383 was also captured on a commercial view-card primarily intended to illustrate Cinderford's Triangle and war memorial. The rear-end view of the bus is interesting as it shows the rear entrance, reached by two deep steps, and a ladder to its right for the conductor to access the roof-top luggage rack.

Shipton Oliffe, Compton Abdale, Andoversford Whittington and Cheltenham.
BUS SERVICE. TIME & FARE TABLE.
Cheltenham Depot, Crown Hotel Yard.

	Daily a.m. Depart	Tuesd'y Thurs'y Satur'y p m.	Tuesd y Thurs'y Satur'y p m.	Thurs'y Satur'y p m.	Satur'y p.m.	Satur'y p.m.	Satur'y p.m.	Sunday p.m.	Sunday p.m.	Sunday p.m.	Fare Table					
SHIPTON OLIFFE	9 55	1 30	3 30	6 30	8 30	10 5	1 25	5 0	9 0		0	2	3	4	6	8
SHIPTON X ROAD	9 57	1 32	3 32	6 32	8 32	10 7	1 27	5 2	9 2		2	0	2	4	6	8
ANDOVERSFORD	10 0	1 35	3 35	6 35	8 35	10 10	1 30	5 5	9 5		3	2	0	2	4	6
WHITTINGTON	10 5	1 40	3 40	6 40	8 40	10 15	1 35	5 10	9 10		4	4	2	0	2	4
VIADUCT	10 10	1 43	3 43	6 43	8 43	10 18	1 38	5 13	9 13		6	6	4	2	0	2
EAST END	10 14	1 46	3 46	6 46	8 46	10 21	1 41	5 16	9 16		8	8	6	4	2	0
CHELTENHAM	10 20	1 55	3 55	6 55	8 55	10 25	1 45	5 22	9 22		9	8	6	6	4	4
Arrive																

	Monday Wedn'y Friday Dep pm	Tuesd'y Thurs'y Satur'y p.m.	Tuesd,y Thurs'y Satur'y p.m.	Tuesd y Thurs'y Satur'y p.m.	Thurs'y p.m.	Satur'y p.m.	Satur'y p.m.	Satur'y p.m.	Sunday p.m.	Sunday p.m	Sunday p.m.
CHELTENHAM	1 10	12 30	2 45	5 15	10 30	8 0	9 30	11 15	3 20	5 30	10 15
EAST END	1 19	12 39	2 54	5 24	10 39	8 9	9 39	11 24	3 26	5 36	10 21
VIADUCT	1 22	12 42	2 57	5 27	10 42	8 12	9 42	11 27	3 28	5 38	10 23
WHITTINGTON	1 25	12 45	3 0	5 30	10 45	8 15	9 45	11 30	3 32	5 43	10 27
ANDOVERSFORD	1 30	12 50	3 5	5 35	10 50	8 17	9 50	11 35	3 37	5 48	10 32
SHIPTON X ROAD	1 33	12 53	3 8	5 38	10 53	8 20	9 53	11 38	3 40	5 51	10 35
SHIPTON OLIFFE	1 35	12 55	3 10	5 40	10 55	8 22	9 55	11 40	3 42	5 53	10 37
Arrive											

COMPTON ABDALE Return from CHELTENHAM
Times as above Fare 1/- Each Way

Children under 3 years Free.   3 years and under 12 Half ordinary fares.   Fraction of 1d counts as 1d.

Every endeavour is made to ensure Punctual Running but this is not guaranteed.

W. PERRETT, Proprietor.

Phone No : Andoversford 44.

Today Perrett's Coaches has a fleet of eight coaches, and is still based in Shipton Oliffe from where the family's carrier's cart used to operate. The company continues to operate the route into Cheltenham. This 1937 timetable was for that route. Andoversford was particularly well served by local bus services, being located at the junction of the A40 and A436. This meant that services from Stow-on-the-Wold, Bourton-on-the-Water, Guiting, Shipton, Northleach and Aldsworth all passed through the small village.

In the 1920s, members of the Silvey family were to resume motor bus operations. Mr C.J. Silvey, trading as the Epney Bus Company, introduced a service to Gloucester in 1922 and, in 1928 added a service from Longney to Stroud. Fiat DD 2416 is seen almost certainly when brand new in April 1923; its body was probably built in Gloucester by Healey's. In the original photograph, just visible along its roof-mounted board, is a list of the main villages served on its route into Gloucester: Frampton, Fretherne, Framilode, Saul, Epney, Longney and Hardwicke. C.J. Silvey sold his bus services to Bristol Tramways in 1932, but he retained a coach for private hire work for a while thereafter. His cousins, Samuel and Felix Silvey, ran their own bus operation from nearby Epney. They ran services from both Frocester and Arlingham into Gloucester. In 1958 the Frocester service was ceded to the Bristol Omnibus Company (as Bristol Tramways had by then become) in return for the bigger company giving up its share of the service to Arlingham. Silveys continued to operate the latter service until selling out in 1969.

Shortly after the First World War, Thomas Perry and Roland Jackson jointly set up a small haulage business in Gloucester. In 1928 they turned their attention to passenger transport and launched an operation under the name of Blue Star Coaches. Four new coaches were acquired and a daily express service to London was introduced. An application was also made to operate some local routes within Gloucester. This, however, did not find favour with the City Council. Blue Star Coaches operated from premises in India Road, where a coach terminal was created. The success of the operation was such that within a year it had been bought out by Red and White Motor Services who continued to use the India Road facilities for some years. The largest vehicle in the Blue Star fleet was this twenty-five-seater Leyland Lioness. FH 5724 was bodied by Strachan.

FH 5398 was the registration of this Blue Star twenty-seat Dennis G. The vehicle was photographed in Worcester Street, Gloucester, with Mr Thomas Perry at the wheel. On this occasion, his passengers included Veronica and Harriett Perry.

Twin of the Dennis was FH 5399, a GMC T20 with twenty-seat Strachan body. The side panels of all the Blue Star vehicles prominently displayed a summary of their route along their sides: Gloucester – Stroud – Reading – London. Departure from Gloucester was at 09.15 each day. There was a ten-minute stop at the Cosy Team Rooms in Wantage and arrival in London's Hammersmith Broadway was scheduled for 14.15. The return journey commenced one hour later.

The railway line between Bourton-on-the-Water and Cheltenham opened in 1881. While most other stations along the line stood in or very near the villages from which they took their names, that at Notgrove stood over a mile away. In order to link the station and village, a pony-and-trap service was introduced by Mrs E. Fluck in 1917. Motorization had arrived by 1929 when a second-hand Ford Model T bus was purchased. In October of the same year this sixteen-seater Chevrolet LQ arrived. Although it had been registered in London – probably by the supplying agent or bodybuilder – UW 4233 is believed to have been bought new.

In 1930 Mrs Fluck purchased another new Chevrolet. DG 2954 was a model U and again had sixteen-seat bodywork, in this case by a coachbuilder known as Real. In both these views, Mrs Fluck's son Albert is seen with the vehicle. Albert and his younger brother Victor were to manage the company following their mother's death. The operation survived until 1983 when Vic Fluck retired and sold the business to Pulham's. In an early example of the advertising slogans, later to become so popular within the industry, emblazoned across the rear of the vehicle was the legend The Notgrove Riviera Saloon!

Little is known of the history of this vehicle, seen while operating for Fluck's. It is a Duple-bodied Bedford WLB dating from the early 1930s. It looks in pristine condition in this view and may well have been acquired new by the operator, despite its Canterbury registration. Fluck's bought out Scarrott's coach business in Stow-on-the-Wold in 1953 and moved their own operations from Notgrove to the former Scarrott premises in Well Lane. Two years later the coach operations of Young's of Stow were also acquired. To consolidate operations a limited company was formed under the name of Luxury (Coaches) Stow Ltd.

A. H. FLUCK'S
NOTGROVE
BUS SERVICE.

Andoversford Sale, Fridays Only.
Route "A"   Notgrove & Cheltenham via Naunton. Hawling Turn & Andoversford.

Outward Service.			Return Service		
Notgrove	Dept. 10 15 a.m.		Cheltenham Plough Yard)	Dept. 3 30 p.m.	
Cold Aston	,, 10 20	.,	East End	,, 3 25	
Bourton-on-the-Water	,, 10 30	.,	Viaduct	,, 3 30	,,
Brockle Clump (Cross Rds)	,, 10 35	,,	Whittington Tur	,, 3 37	,,
Naunton (Black Horse)	,, 10 40	.,	Andoversford	,, 3 40	,,
Fox Hill (Inn)	,, 10 45	,,	Salperton Turn	,, 3 53	,,
Hawling & Notgrove Turn	,. 10 50	,,	Hawling & Notgrove Turn	,, 3 55	,.
Salperton Turn	,, 10 52	,,	Fox Hill (Inn)	,, 3 58	,,
Andoversford	,. 11 10	,,	Naunton (Black Horse)	,, 4 5	,,
Whittington Turn	,. 11 13	,,	Brockle Clump (Cross Rds)	,, 4 10	
Viaduct	,, 11 20	.,	Bourton-on-the Water	,, 4 15	,,
East End	, 11 25	,,	Cold Aston	,, 4 20	,,
Cheltenham (Plough Yard) Arr	11 30	,.	Notgrove	Arr. 4 25	,,

One of several services which Fluck's operated was that from their base at Notgrove to Cheltenham, taking a circuitous route via Bourton and Naunton. The return fare to Cheltenham in the 1930s was 1s 9d.

Mr E.C. Young traded as Cotswold Coaches from his garage at Stow-on-the-Wold. Five of the coaches he bought in the late 1920s and 1930s were of Dodge manufacture. One of these vehicles is seen when new. It was photographed at the Tyler and Martin coach-building works in Cheltenham. Despite its small size, two passenger doors were fitted. Note also the 'sunshine' roof. The full width fold-down hoods of earlier years were by now a thing of the past.

Cotswold Coaches also bought two Reos. DG 2109 was a model FB and had carried a twenty-seater body by Thurgood. It was sold in 1936, but very many years later, when reduced to a chassis, it returned to the county. It is seen here in a yard in Gloucester's dock-land in 1976. It is thought to have been scrapped soon afterwards. Cotswold Coaches introduced a service from Stow-on-the-Wold to Cheltenham in 1929 and this was soon extended to Moreton-in-Marsh. The service was acquired by Kearsey's Coaches of Cheltenham in 1951, but eventually passed to Pulhams. The remainder of the Cotswold coaching business was sold to the Fluck family in 1955.

Mr Sydney Sperry of Cheltenham was a keen cyclist and went on to win many trophies for his success in cycling competitions. It was therefore not surprising that, rather than entering the family sign-writing business, he opened a cycle shop in Cheltenham High Street. He was selling cycles and accessories as well as undertaking repairs. Mr Sperry's enthusiasm and hard work helped create a successful business and, a few years later, he decided to expand. The business moved to premises on the opposite side of the High Street, again providing a small shop area. This time, however, there was also a large workshop to the rear of the shop. The business continued to meet the needs of the cycling community. Moreover, now that more space was available, the shop was able to offer a daily parking facility for those cycling into the town from outlying districts. The garage could easily accommodate half a dozen cars and a full motor repair service was introduced. The business traded under the name of Cotswold Garage. Early additions to the range of services were petrol sales and the provision of private hire cars, several of which were available either for regular contracts or for weddings or other special occasions. It was undoubtedly the success of car hire which led Mr Sperry to acquire coaches. The date of their introduction is not certain, but it appears to have been at the end of the 1920s. About ten coaches were operated over the years, the largest being thirty-two-seater Bedfords OWBs in the immediate post-war years. It was just possible to park two of the coaches nose-to-tail in the entrance to the garage which is clearly visible to right of centre in this view. Mr Sperry sold out in 1948 and the premises were acquired by the Marchant family who went on to develop their own coach business from the same site. Although the High Street site was sold in 1972, the Marchant operation continues today with more than twenty coaches currently in service.

The Saloon 'Bus
Plough Garage, Ford,
Broadway.
T. Bowles, Proprietor.

Mr Thomas Bowles of Ford, near Temple Guiting, was an early operator of buses in the Cotswolds. The earliest-known vehicle was a fourteen-seater Daimler, probably a lorry/bus, acquired in 1920, but the chassis of which dated from 1910. Here a Ford Model T, believed to have been DD 3185 of August 1923, is seen in an advertising postcard. Bowles' garage stood alongside the Plough Inn at Ford and the family ran coaches from the same site until 1991. Members of the Bowles family ran The Plough and also had local farming interests. A haulage operation, with particular emphasis in the earlier years on the movement of livestock, was also developed. This is yet another example of a bus operation that is just one aspect of a multi-faceted family-run business portfolio so typical of transport pioneers. Thomas Bowles' son David provided several of the views included in this volume and had offered to assist in providing detailed captions for those to be published; sadly his sudden death occurred before that task could be undertaken.

DD 8783 was a Reo G delivered to Bowles' Coaches in January 1926. These views were taken at Ford soon after the twenty-seater had been delivered. Note that the header tank of the radiator unusually stands several inches higher than the top of the bonnet. The lettering above the front of the running board gives details of the maximum permissible loading on each of the axles. Reo was a US manufacturer, established by Mr R.E. Olds, from whose initials it took its name. Many Reos were imported into the UK in the 1920s.

Bowles quickly developed a regular service operation. Two services ran to Evesham and two into Cheltenham, via very different routes. One travelled via Stanway and Alderton and the other via Temple Guiting and Andoversford. The Cheltenham services survived for many years and were eventually taken over by A.H. Kearsey from that town in 1951. The service to Alderton, although no longer running on to Stanway, is still maintained today by Kearsey's successor, Marchant's Coaches. This 1928 Chevrolet LO fourteen-seater gave three and a half year's service to the company, about as much as would realistically have been expected from a lightweight vehicle of this type in use nearly every day.

Bowles purchased two more Reos in 1929. DF 8473 arrived in August of that year and was a model FAA with twenty-seat coach body. The vehicle alongside appears to be another of Bowles but it has not been possible to identify it.

Bowles received their first Bedford in July 1932. DG 4933 was a twenty-seater Duple-bodied WLB. Although fitted out as a service bus, the vehicle's destination blind suggests that it may have been out with a private party when photographed. The distinction between buses and coaches was not great; in many cases it was limited to the form of seating, coaches generally having higher backed and more generously upholstered seats.

Bedford revamped their W-series goods and passenger models in 1938; the vertical bars of the radiator stone guards were replaced by a more rounded 'bull nose' with horizontal bars. This anticipated the K, M and O models which replaced the W range in 1939, and continued in production until 1952 after a war-time break. Bowles' DDF 669 was one such face-lifted vehicle, arriving at Ford in March 1939. Anyone familiar with the Cotswolds will recognise the setting of this viewcard as Bourton-on-the-Water. The driver is well turned-out. White coats tended not to be used in small companies after the war. The vehicle has standard Duple twenty-six-seat coachwork. Many Bedford passenger chassis had Duple bodywork; the two concerns, both based in Hendon, worked closely together to develop new designs, although neither company was governed by an exclusivity agreement.

From the carrier's cart depicted earlier, Pulham's introduced motor vehicles in the 1920s. This Chevrolet X-type was believed to have been their first. DF 1915 was new in March 1927 and carried a fourteen-seat body by Williams of Cheltenham. Like many of these early vehicles, a luggage rack was provided on the roof – in this case a ladder was permanently fitted to the rear of the vehicle to facilitate access. The photograph was almost certainly taken when the vehicle was new. The railway line in the background is probably the Great Western line somewhere between Andoversford and Kingham junctions.

This interior view of DF 1915 gives a good indication of the layout of a 1920s fourteen-seater and of the standards of comfort which could be expected of rural buses of the time.

Two more Chevrolets quickly followed. Here DF 1915 stands with DF 2695 and DF 6116 of 1927 and 1928 respectively. All had Williams fourteen-seat bodies. Mr Williams later joined with a Mr Bayliss to further develop his successful coach-building business in Cheltenham; however few coaches were made as their skills were generally applied to the construction of car bodies and accident repair work. The two newer Chevrolets were models LM and LP. The progression of the chassis designation letters indicated the continual refinement of the 30cwt Chevrolet chassis. On the original print the destination 'Northleach Grammar School' is visible above the windscreens on each of the vehicles. School services are nothing new, although it is only in much more recent times, with greater centralisation of educational facilities, that they have become such a major commitment for most rural coach operators. Note how bodies had suddenly become much wider; while that on DF 1915 is little wider than the rear axle, those on DF 6116, and even more noticeably on the earlier view of Bowles' DF 5407, show a marked excess over the axle width.

Something different in the Pulham fleet was a 1930 Dodge, DF 9863. Its body was by Healey of Gloucester. The photograph was taken at the Pulham farm in Naunton.

Bedfords supplanted Chevrolets in 1931. The first two Bedford PSVs arrived in Gloucestershire in May of that year and in June Pulham's received their first example. DG 2721 was a Bedford WLG, the G indicating that it was a goods vehicle chassis; the bus variant (the WLB)was not launched until later that year. It was delivered as a chassis only and the body was sourced separately. The body may have been transferred from an earlier vehicle, but as this was a twenty-seater that seems unlikely, as earlier vehicles were smaller and a major rebuild would have been necessary. Note the clip-on destination board for Cheltenham and a sticker advertising the Tidworth Tattoo. Just visible is lettering indicating an unladen weight of 2.5 tons and a speed limit of 30mph.

A vehicle which was to remain unique in the Pulham fleet, with respect to both chassis and body builders, was AAD 140. This was a Commer B3 whose bodywork had been built by the Gloucester Railway Carriage & Wagon works. The B3 was a new model in the Commer range and the forward control variant had been designed specifically with passenger applications in mind. AAD 140 was delivered in December 1934. Its twenty-six seats were contained in a rather angular body. While no repeat orders were placed, the vehicle gave almost ten years of service to the Naunton operator, before moving north for further service in Yorkshire. In addition to their core business of constructing railway rolling stock, GRCW built a variety of vehicles over the years, including horse buses and tramcars. Of particular note was the building, in conjunction with Watts of Lydney, of both chassis and bodies for nine Gloster Gardner motor coaches in the early 1930s. Six of these entered service with Red and White and the other three went to other operators in South Wales.

Messrs Richings and Battershall were in business in Staunton for some years, until the late 1940s. The business began when Mr Richings acquired a pony and trap for local delivery work. George Battershall began working for him on an occasional basis, but soon acquired a stake in the business, which then rapidly expanded. By the later 1930s around a dozen goods vehicles were in use, primarily on milk collection duties; the haulage business was nationalised in 1948. Motor coaches had appeared by the late 1920s and services were introduced between Gloucester and Ledbury, and Gloucester and Tewkesbury via Maisemore and Tirley. The former was quickly acquired by Bristol Tramways, but the latter route continued for some years. The coach business was sold to Bayliss of Dymock in 1947. Here DF 4929 is seen outside the White Horse Inn in Ledbury. Note the smartly dressed passengers, the ladies wearing carnations and the lady standing in the centre alongside the white-coated driver carrying a bouquet – clearly they were in the town for in an important celebration. The vehicle was a Dennis E-type, new in April 1928, and carried a thirty-two-seat body. (Photo: J C Smith & Son, Ledbury)

Another Richings and Battershall vehicle is seen here with an even larger party. DG 4038 was a Leyland Tiger LT5, with a thirty-two-seat Harrington body. It was new in March 1932 and served in the fleet until 1947, when it moved to a Lancashire operator. The Seven Stars in Ledbury's Homend provides the background for this mid-1930s view. Vehicles were now remaining serviceable for rather more years than the earlier generations, which frequently saw little more than five or six years of use. This new found longevity reflected improvements both in construction techniques and road maintenance. Standing behind the R&B coach is another Leyland, BAD 854 of the Warner's fleet from Tewkesbury. (Photo: J C Smith & Son, Ledbury)

Following war service in the Middle East, Mr Reginald Dingle moved from his native Cornwall to settle in Quenington, as a groom for a local landowner. His work took him regularly to London where he became acquainted with staff at a motor agency. This kindled his interest in motoring and led him to acquire vehicles of his own. He took over his own farm in Quenington later in the 1920s and began running buses, like so many others in rural areas, as a sideline to his main occupation. His main commitment was in providing the daily service through the Coln Valley, between Quenington and Cirencester. This view is dated by the family to around 1930, and shows Mr Dingle alongside what appears to be a new Chevrolet fourteen-seat service bus. It is almost certainly DG 2964, a Chevrolet Model U, which was new in July 1931.

Just a year later a further service bus arrived in Quenington. This was a twenty-seater Bedford WLB. DG 4313 is seen in its home village. Dingle's coach business was acquired by Marchants of Cheltenham in 1954.

In 1936 Mr Dingle acquired a twenty-six-seater coach, primarily to support the excursions from Quenington, for which a licence had been obtained in 1934. Registered BDF 273, this was one of Bedford's new WTB models, the passenger-carrying version of their 3-ton goods model. The vehicle was bodied by Willmott. The photograph above shows the vehicle in Quenington in September 1937. The photograph below was taken in Dingle's garage some sixty years later! When the business was sold this coach, then eighteen years old, was retained with the intention of its body being removed and the chassis used for the basis of a truck for use on the family's farm. That conversion never took place and the vehicle remained stored under cover for forty-four years, still displaying its 1954 road fund licence! It was sold soon afterwards and is currently being restored.

Mr F.H. Munn of Cinderford operated two Model T Ford charabancs in the early 1920s. As may be seen from this view the vehicles were particularly basic in their design – but doubtless they did the job for which they were intended. This is thought to have been AD 8198, new in 1921. Her Sister vehicle AD 9354 of 1922 later passed to another early Cinderford operator, Rowlinson.

A later Rowlinson vehicle was this Bedford WLB, with twenty-seat Duple coach body. It was later acquired by Mr Percy Grindle for use on his Forest Greyhound Tours, and then passed to his brother Roy Grindle, all three companies operating from Cinderford. This photograph was probably taken during its time with Forest Greyhound. The vehicle dated from the early 1930s.

In November 1928 Forest Greyhound purchased this twenty-seater Dodge coach, DF 6155. Its all-male party exhibit a wide variety of dress standards – some are casually dressed (for the 1930s) but at least two are wearing bow ties! Mr Grindle, wearing a trilby hat, sits alongside the driver. The Dodge spent about five years in the fleet before passing to Mr Wilfred Parry of Littledean who used it to transport miners to the Eastern United and Lightmoor Collieries.

A more substantial coach in the Forest Greyhound fleet was this Dennis G-type twenty-seater. FH 5515 was bought new by Davis & Sons of Gloucester in 1928, but passed on to Grindles in about 1930. The name of Grindle has been associated with Cinderford transport for over a century. Mr Harry Grindle senior used his father's horses to provide a Saturday cab service to Gloucester in the early twentieth century; his two sons, Roy and Percy, were to introduce motor vehicles some twenty-five years later. Grindle's Coaches lives on, run by Phillip Grindle and his father Harry, son of Roy. Four generations have been involved in the evolution of transport in the Forest town.

To promote his Forest Greyhound coaches, Percy Grindle produced this advertising card in the 1930s, depicting two of his most recent vehicles, both posed in the Forest. Top right is Gilford GJ 5770, a 168OT model – the 'OT' denoting Over Type, or forward control. Along with its twin, 5771, this vehicle arrived in Cinderford in 1932 when little more than a year old. They had previously served with a London operator, Blue and White Coaches. Both had London Lorries thirty-two-seat bodies; they remained at work in Cinderford until 1944. Gilford, based in High Wycombe, was another manufacturer of quality coach chassis who succumbed to the intense competition of the early 1930s. The other vehicle is a Bedford WTB, with twenty-six-seat Duple body, in this case fitted out to a particularly high specification. BAD 428 was bought new by Forest Greyhound in February 1936. Note that it was fitted with a rear entrance door; by that time most operators were specifying forward entrances for new coaches. This, along with the Dingle vehicle on page 97, illustrates the original styling of the WTB as introduced in 1935, with the flat and vertically slatted radiator grille. One of the original WTB demonstrators, with chassis number 2, was snapped up by Scarrott of Stow-on-the-Wold when it became surplus to Bedford's needs; it was registered BAD 288. The use of publicity postcards was at one time quite popular.

This is the other Gilford, GJ 5771, captured on a rather dismal day. There are signs of recent rain and the luggage on the roof-mounted rack has been sheeted over. The passengers too are wearing their rain gear. There is not a man in sight – presumably the ladies were 'escaping' for a few days. Note that the front door slides, while that at the rear is hinged, swinging outwards. The setting appears to be Woodside Road in Cinderford. The garages for both of the Grindle businesses were in that same road for many years, and it was only in the mid-1990s that the remaining Grindle business moved to more spacious premises on the Forest Vale industrial estate. Percy Grindle diversified his transport interests as the years went by, acquiring a fleet of cars for use at weddings and funerals and also several furniture removal vans.

Percy's brother Roy was also buying quality coaches during the 1930s – this post-war view shows Dennis Lancet BAD 625. The coach was delivered new in March 1936, fitted with a thirty-seven-seat Willowbrook body. It was in the fleet for twenty-two years. How different this vehicle was to the Cinderford delivery of fifteen years earlier. After years of concentrating on specialist goods vehicle production Dennis made a return to the production of bus chassis in the later years of the twentieth century.

Mr William Ives expanded his motor engineering business in Tetbury by branching out into coaching in the 1920s. His first known vehicle was an Overland fourteen-seater bought new in 1925. From an early stage he adopted the trading name of Ivory Coaches. Stage services were operated from Tetbury to both Cirencester and Bristol. About ten vehicles had passed through the fleet in the years before the Second World War. These were a mixed bunch, but several were Guys, a make not otherwise covered within these pages. Among them was this Guy Conquest which was bought new in November 1933. It was fitted with a bus body seating thirty-two. The vehicle did not last long, passing on to Vaughan of Chippenham in Wiltshire in 1938. It was photographed during its eleven year stay in the Vaughan fleet. Its headlamps are masked and its front wing tips painted white, thus indicating that the photograph was taken during the war years. Its relatively early departure from Tetbury was probably attributable to the sale in 1935 of the stage services to Bristol Tramways. Ivory Coaches built up a modern coaching fleet in the post-war years and was taken over by the relatively short-lived Ladvale group in 1975.

TIME TABLE

Sunday and Week-day Services

TETBURY - CIRENCESTER

		WEEK-DAYS			SUNDAYS	
		A.M.	P.M.	P.M.	P.M.	P.M.
TETBURY	(dep.)	**8-20**	**2-35**	**8-0**	**1-20**	**7-55**
TROUBLE HOUSE		8-25	2-40	8-5	1-25	8-0
CULKERTON	...	8-30	2-45	8-10	1-30	8-5
RODMARTON	...	8-35	2-50	8-15	1-35	8-10
KEMBLE	...	8-40	2-55	8-20	1-40	8-15
CIRENCESTER	(arr.)	**8-45**	**3-0**	**8-25**	**1-45**	**8-20**

		WEEK-DAYS			SUNDAYS	
		A.M.	P.M.	P.M.	P.M.	P.M.
CIRENCESTER	(dep.)	**8-50**	**3-50**	**10·25**	**1-50**	**8-35**
KEMBLE		8-55	3-55	10-30	1-55	8-40
RODMARTON	...	9-0	4-0	10-35	2-0	8-45
CULKERTON	...	9-5	4-5	10-40	2-5	8-50
TROUBLE HOUSE		9-10	4-10	10-45	2-10	8-55
TETBURY	(arr.)	**9-15**	**4-15**	**10·50**	**2-15**	**9-0**

TETBURY - CHIPPING SODBURY - BRISTOL

		WEEK-DAYS		SUNDAYS
		A.M.	P.M.	P.M.
TETBURY	(dep.)	**9-20**	**4-20**	**2-20**
BEVERSTON	...	9-25	4-25	2-25
CALCUT	...	9-30	4-30	2-30
LASBOROUGH	...	9-33	4-33	2-33
LEIGHTERTON	...	9-36	4-36	2-36
TRESHAM	...	9-39	4-39	2-39
HAWKESBURY	...	9-46	4-46	2-46
DUNKIRK	...	9-49	4-49	2-49
HORTON CORNER		9-54	4-54	2-54
HORTON	...	9-58	4-58	2-58
CHIPPING SODBURY		10-13	5-13	3-13
YATE	...	10-18	5-18	3-18
MAYS HILL	...	10-20	5-20	3-20
COALPIT HEATH	...	10-25	5-25	3-25
KENDLESHIRE	...	10-28	5-28	3-28
DOWNEND	...	10-33	5-33	3-33
FISHPONDS		10-38	5-38	3-38
BRISTOL	... (arr.)	**10-53**	**5-53**	**3-53**

		WEEK-DAYS		SUNDAYS
		P.M.	P.M.	P.M.
BRISTOL	... (dep.)	**1-0**	**6-20**	**6-20**
FISHPONDS	...	1-15	6-35	6-35
DOWNEND	...	1-20	6-40	6-40
KENDLESHIRE	...	1-25	6-45	6-45
COALPIT HEATH	...	1-28	6-48	6-48
MAYS HILL	...	1-31	6-51	6-51
YATE	... ...	1-35	6-55	6-55
CHIPPING SODBURY		1-40	7-0	7-0
HORTON	...	1-55	7-15	7-15
HORTON CORNER		1-59	7-19	7-19
DUNKIRK	... ...	2-4	7-24	7-24
HAWKESBURY	...	2-7	7-26	7-26
TRESHAM	... ...	2-14	7-34	7-34
LEIGHTERTON	...	2-18	7-38	7-38
LASBOROUGH	...	2-21	7-41	7-41
CALCUT	... ...	2-24	7-44	7-44
BEVERSTON	...	2-30	7-50	7-50
TETBURY	... (arr.)	**2-35**	**7-55**	**7-55**

W. IVES, TETBURY.   Phone 12

Taylor & Sons, Printers, Hincly, Wilts.

The 1934 time-table for Ives' Coaches services from Tetbury to Cirencester and Bristol.

DDG 393 was another of the face-lifted Bedford WTBs – 'WTB2s' as they are known, albeit unofficially, by some. It was again fitted with standard Duple twenty-six-seat coachwork and was delivered to Ellis & Bull of Moreton-in-Marsh in June 1939. Amazingly, the vehicle survived with E&B for thirty years, not being withdrawn until April 1969, by which time it was the last remaining pre-war coach at work in the county. Tom Ellis and Arthur Bull had purchased the two coach business of Percy Sheen of Moreton in the mid-1930s; the setting up of the RAF base at Moreton during the war years brought them sufficient work to increase the fleet to five coaches. This WTB is now in the safe hands of a preservationist. Although E&B were registered under the name of the Railway Garage Company, none of the vehicles appear to have displayed this trading name – derived from the proximity of their garage to Moreton's railway station. That garage is the setting for these two views taken in 1964.

Development of bus services within the Stroud Valleys is particularly complex – the Great Western Railway and the National Omnibus company both played an important part, but their contribution is beyond the scope of this volume. John Merritt of Minchinhampton, trading as Grey Motors, progressed from the lorry bus depicted in Chapter 3 to a small fleet of Chevrolets purchased during the final years of the 1920s. Services were operated linking Minchinhampton, Avening, Tetbury, Nailsworth and Malmesbury with Stroud. Within the same time frame Australian Nicholas Reyne, posted as a serviceman to Aston Down during the First World War, settled in the area and commenced bus operation in 1927, purchasing the Red Bus operations of a Mr Whittingham the following year. He started an express service from Stroud to London that same year and extended it to Gloucester a few months later. It is believed that Mr Reyne bought into Merritt's business at an early opportunity, but the two businesses operated as semi-independent units until 1932 when Red Bus Services Ltd was formed to take the combined operation forward. In 1934 the company, with some thirty-five vehicles, was purchased by Red and White Services whose origins lay in the Forest of Dean and the Monmouthshire valleys. By that time the local National Omnibus operations had become Western National and the latter co-existed in Stroud with Red and White until 1950. In that year Red and White was nationalised, joining Western National in public ownership. Rationalisation and territorial adjustments saw both operators hand their services in the Stroud area over to Bristol Tramways later that year. Bristol Tramways updated its name to Bristol Omnibus in 1955 and its operations in Gloucestershire were transferred to the newly formed Cheltenham & Gloucester Omnibus Company in 1983 in the run up to privatisation. Cheltenham & Gloucester sold out to Stagecoach in 1993, thus bringing yet another major operating group onto the Stroud bus scene. The local operating name of Stroud Valleys was introduced in 1983 for vehicles based in that town and continues today. One of Reyne's earliest vehicles was this eighteen-seat Chevrolet LM. DF 3269 was new in 1927. Driver Arthur Hill was photographed outside Minchinhampton Market House.

The Red Bus Company launched its express service from Stroud to London in 1928. For its inauguration this Thornycroft A6 joined the fleet in March of that year. The vehicle had a twenty-seat dual door body by Hall Lewis and was presented at its best for this publicity postcard. The emblem on the side panels of DF 4605 depicts the company logo – a kangaroo, reflecting Mr Reyne's Australian roots. Around the motif are the words Red Bus Company, Austral Garage, Stroud. Austral Garage was in Lansdown. The Thornycroft is seen below speeding past the junction of Butterow Hill and the Rodborough Road as it heads for

Minchinhampton in around 1930. It was on its way to London, possibly on the mid-afternoon departure from Stroud.

Delivered at the same time as the Thornycroft, March 1928, was this Chevrolet LO fourteen-seater coach. DF 4607 is seen here alongside a 1927 Bean tourer. The location is not known.

This GMC T20 fourteen-seater was delivered new to Reyne in July 1928. Regular driver Frank Powell is seen with his vehicle at the College Cricket Ground in Cheltenham when the vehicle was still in its first flush of operations. The vehicle was regularly deployed on a Bakers' Mill-Chalford feeder service, via narrow lanes, connecting with the main Stroud service at Chalford. It was parked overnight at the Central Garage at Chalford.

Such was the success of the London service that it was extended to start from Gloucester within months of commencing and justified the purchase of two Leyland Tigers in 1929: DF 6916 and DF 9186. Both had been bodied by the rather unfortunately named London Lorries company and seated twenty-six. The route ran via Cirencester, Wantage and Reading with two departures each day. DF 9186 is seen outside the Red Bus offices in Upper George Street, Stroud with passengers ready to board. Inspector Les Grimmett was on hand to supervise the departure. These vehicles were the last word in passenger comfort; but although styling gradually evolved, keeping pace with the design fashions of the day, very few real advances were made in the interior appointment of coaches for another twenty-five years.

Following page: The Red Bus company issued this leaflet to publicise details of its Gloucester-London service for the 1933/34 winter season.

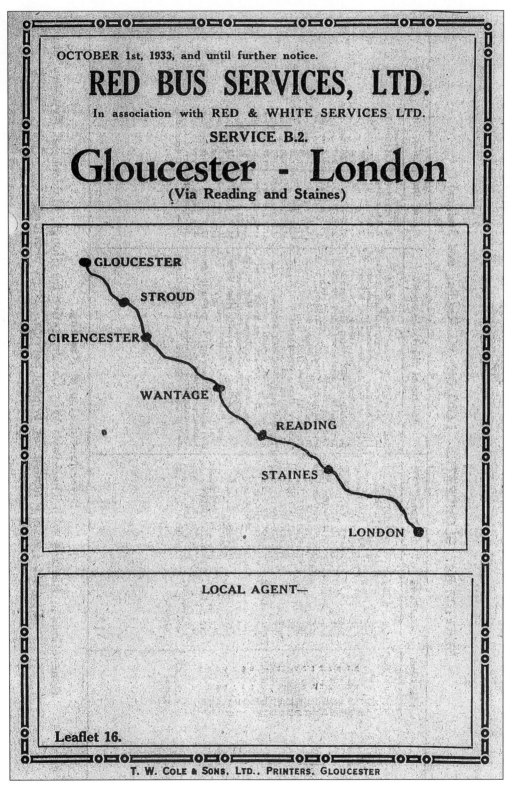

OCTOBER 1st, 1933, and until further notice.

RED BUS SERVICES, LTD.

In association with RED & WHITE SERVICES LTD.

SERVICE B.2.

Gloucester - London

(Via Reading and Staines)

GLOUCESTER

STROUD

CIRENCESTER

WANTAGE

READING

STAINES

LONDON

LOCAL AGENT—

Leaflet 16.

T. W. COLE & SONS, LTD., PRINTERS, GLOUCESTER

This GMC was delivered to Reyne one month after that illustrated on page 105. The body on DF 5974 was, however, by a different coachbuilder. It is seen here outside the Riflemans at Slad in about 1930. Standing alongside are, from left to right, driver Bill Bourne, fitter Arthur Burrows and driver Charlie Rudge.

DF 5987 was new in 1928 to another Stroud operator, a Mr Cox. This fourteen-seater Chevrolet LP joined the Reyne fleet in 1930. It was used on the service from Stroud to France Lynch via Chalford Hill, Bussage and Eastcombe. It was photographed in Jubilee Terrace, Brownshill with driver Martin Smart. The bus was kept in Mr Smart's quarry at Chalford Hill overnight.

The small vehicle to the extreme right of this view is a twelve-seater bus on a Morris T chassis. Although the vehicle may appear to be an insignificant part of the photograph, it nevertheless presents the Morris in its correct setting – at the disposal of hotel guests. A number of larger hotels ran small buses in the years up to 1930 – and indeed it is not unknown today, although today's minibuses are more often used for staff transport. In their original role the buses were used for meeting guests from local railway stations, and for providing excursions for small private parties. The Bear Inn at Rodborough was the subject of this commercial view card. The Inn was run by Major Henry Rowlatt and in 1924-25 he purchased four buses: two Vulcans and a pair of Morris's of which DD 6205 is seen here. In addition to meeting the needs of the hotel, he put his buses to work on a public service from nearby Minchinhampton into Stroud. So successful was this service that it led to the Stroud branch of the National Omnibus company buying out the Rowlatt bus operation in 1926.

It has not been possible to fully identify all of the photographs I have acquired. Nevertheless, even without full identification, the images contribute effectively to the essence of these early days of motor bus operations. This charabanc was allegedly photographed in the Malvern Hills having conveyed a party from Mitcheldean. The date was almost certainly early 1920s. The vehicle is a Karrier B80 four-tonner and it appears to have a full complement of thirty-two enthusiastic passengers on board. It was customary for charabanc parties to pause for a group photograph. This was both a reflection of the novelty value of such trips at the time, and a consequence of the vehicles offering an ideal platform on which photographers could compose a view of the whole of the party. The move to enclosed vehicles largely brought an end to this practice.

Like a number of others in this book relating to his beloved Stroud area, this photograph was provided by Mr Stanley Gardiner when I was at an early stage in thinking about the preparation of this historical record. Along with Lionel Padin, Mr Gardiner had built up an impressive photographic archive covering all aspects of life in Stroud and its valleys. His enthusiasm and encouragement certainly helped me in my task and it is particularly sad that he is unable to see this completed work. Mr Gardiner's records show that this party was travelling from the Stroud area in the early 1920s. The date would certainly appear to be correct for this basic solid-tyred Commer. All twenty-eight of the passengers were females, and all of them be-hatted. Most had managed to put on a smile, but a few appeared to be unsure whether this was quite the proper thing to do!

This vehicle is thought to be the larger of two Dennis charabancs operated by the Gloucester Co-operative Society. If so, it was registered FH 2245 and was new in January 1921. Note that, as was required, the maximum permissible load weights for each axle are declared on the side of the vehicle: 2tons 2cwt 1qr on the front axle and 4tons 4cwt 2qrs on the rear. The vehicle's unladen weight is also shown as 4tons 4cwt. Simple arithmetic indicates that this allows about twelve stone for each person and their luggage. The Co-op vehicle operated under the name *Pride of The West*. Both Co-op vehicles were licensed as lorries at various times of their lives; it is possible that the bodies were demountable.

At least two photographs exist of this late 1920s vehicle in the same location, with different parties on board. Both were taken when leaving Gloucester at the start of day trips. The legend on its side panel describes it as a Low Level Safety Coach, a slogan used not to declare that the coach was offering only a low level of safety (!) but to indicate that vehicles were being constructed with lower slung chassis frames, lowering the centre of gravity and providing greater stability. Within the motif is the lettering H&A, the significance of which remains a mystery.

Mr Eddie Jones of Hunger Hill, Dursley was another motor bus pioneer, although it is thought that he never had more than one or two vehicles at any one time. In 1928 he took this party of twenty-seven Dursley folk on a day trip to Cheddar Gorge, where they paused for this photograph. The type of vehicle has not been identified – might it have been a Star Flyer or an AJS Pilot?

Another party from Dursley visited Weston-Super-Mare and Cheddar in September 1929. Here they are in Cheddar. The driver had the company of thirty-two passengers in a vehicle yet to be identified.

The term 'charabanc' is often used to refer to all early single-deck buses and coaches; those more closely involved in the recording of vehicle types, normally use the term to refer only to those vehicles where a separate access is provided for each row of seats, thereby avoiding the need for a central gangway running the length of the vehicle. By this definition, few charabancs were manufactured after the mid-1920s. This vehicle is believed to have been Thornycroft LB FH 4875, delivered new to a Mr Jones of Gloucester in May 1927. The photograph must have been taken before delivery as the vehicle carries neither registration nor Hackney plates. It does however carry Glevum Glory signwriting, declaring a speed limit of 12mph. After a couple of years the vehicle passed to Mr E.P. Lewis of Frampton-on-Severn, who traded as Blue Bird Services. Blue Bird services ran from Frampton to both Stroud and Gloucester; the service to Stroud was taken over by National Omnibus in 1925, and Bristol Tramways bought out the company, including the Gloucester service, in 1932. The Thornycroft finished its life as a lorry in the Tuffley area of Gloucester. Mr Jones had no further vehicles.

This Time Table is for personal use ONLY, and must not be exhibited for duration of the war.

GILLETT'S
SALOON BUS SERVICE
BETWEEN
WINCHCOMBE
AND
CROWN HOTEL YARD
CHELTENHAM. (Daily)

APPROVED TIME TABLE.

	Depart Gretton Road	Depart Abbey Terrace	Depart Crown Hotel Yard Cheltenham
Sunday	1.55 p.m. 5.45 ,, 9.0 ,,	2.0 p.m. 5.55 ,, 9.15 ,,	2.45 p.m. 6.45 ,, 10.0 ,,
Monday) Tuesday } Friday)	9.35 a.m. 2.10 p.m.	9.45 a.m. 2.15 p.m.	12.30 p.m. 6.0 ,,
Wednesday	9.35 a.m.	9.45 a.m.	1.0 p.m.
Thursday	9.35 a.m. 2.10 p.m. 6.30 ,,	9.45 a.m. 2.15 p.m. 6.45 ,,	12.30 p.m. 6.0 ,, 10.45 ,,
Saturday	9.35 a.m. 2.10 p.m. 6.30 ,,	9.45 a.m. 2.15 p.m. 6.45 ,, 10.0 ,,	12.30 p.m. 6.0 ,, 9.15 ,, ~~11.0~~ 10,45

FARES.

Gilletts of Winchcombe was originally a horse bus operator. This was the timetable for their Cheltenham service during the Second World War. Note the caveat drawing attention to the prohibition of material such as this, giving details of local transport arrangements, being exhibited during the war years

Gillett's Coaches

Proprietors A. W. & E. M. Gillett

COACHES FOR HIRE

— CAR FOR HIRE —

Gretton Road, Winchcombe, Glos.

Telephone Winchcombe 436

Five

The War Years

With effect from 1940 production capacity in engineering plants throughout the country was fully committed to meeting the needs of the war effort. Truck and bus manufacturing plants worked at full capacity to meet the unprecedented needs of the armed forces, generally in the form of trucks and armoured vehicles, but also in some cases turning out aircraft and other military hardware. It was not until 1942 that a limited supply of vehicles became available once more for civilian users. These were models built to strict utility standards, to designs approved by the Ministry of War Transport, and only available to those civilian users who had obtained the necessary Ministry permit. To qualify for such permits operators had to demonstrate that the vehicle was essential for the operation of public services, or for the transport of workers to factories whose production was directly supporting the war effort. The standard single-deck vehicle supplied to rural operators under this scheme was the Bedford OWB; it carried a rather angular body fitted with thirty-two slatted wooden seats. The bodies were built to a standard design by four body builders, although by far the biggest share came from the Duple factory at Hendon. The first two such vehicles in the country were supplied to Gloucestershire operator Roy Grindle of Cinderford for transporting workers from the Forest of Dean to the factories of the Gloster Aircraft Company in Brockworth. In all some eighty of these Bedfords were delivered to local operators between June 1942 and November 1945. Apart from a couple of Austins and a Daimler double-deck, required by Cottrell's for their busy service into Gloucester, no other new vehicles were received by the county's independent operators during the war years.

Almost all of the Bedfords had more comfortable seats fitted as peace returned, capacities being reduced to twenty-eight or thirty in the process. However, their utilitarian construction resulted in most of these vehicles having very short passenger-carrying lives. Some had new coach bodies fitted, but most quickly found new homes as mobile shops, fairground vehicles or as transport for construction staff, as the post-war building boom got under way. Very few photographs seem to have been taken of these vehicles – no doubt a consequence of the combined effects of wartime restrictions and their relatively short periods of service in the county.

Standing alongside the war memorial in this early 1950s view of Moreton-in-Marsh High Street is FAD 498, a Duple-bodied Bedford OWB, delivered new to Ellis & Bull of Moreton in November 1943. The vehicle would almost certainly have been allocated to E&B to enable the company to maintain its service to Stratford-upon-Avon. The Bedford was sold in 1952, but the company continued in business until it sold out to Barry's Coaches in 1975.

COACHES FOR HIRE   DISTANCE NO OBJECT

TERMS MODERATE

THE RAILWAY GARAGE CO.
(A. J. BULL · W. T. ELLIS)

NEW ROAD · MORETON-IN-MARSH · TELEPHONE ♪98

Although, rather oddly, never displayed on the vehicles, Ellis & Bull's letter head made prominent reference to the name of The Railway Garage Co.

Meek's of Nailbridge were allocated a utility Bedford, in order to maintain their service between Ruardean and Cinderford. The vehicle is seen in the early post-war years with Mrs Meek standing alongside. It was supplied through Prailles, the Bedford dealer in Hereford, and was registered in that county as CVJ 336. Note the small diameter of the wartime headlamps.

Meeks later acquired several more utility Bedfords, one of which was FDD 335 purchased in 1948 from Edwards Coaches of nearby Joy's Green. In this view is Mr Albert Meek's son, Derek, who has generously provided a number of items for inclusion in this volume. Both photographs on this page were taken at Meek's garage in Nailbridge.

Mr Vic Fluck stands between two of his mother's coaches, both displaying their masked headlamps. On the left is a Leyland Tiger TS3, which arrived with the Notgrove operator in 1938. It was a 1930 vehicle, but with a later thirty-one-seat coach body fitted. On the right is BAY 756, a Bedford WTB with Duple twenty-six-seat coach body, bought by Mrs Fluck in October 1939 when it was only a year old. To improve their visibility many vehicles had their bumpers and skirts painted white during the war years, although there were, unsurprisingly, many accidents during the blackout.

Cecil Warners' business in Tewkesbury had become firmly established during the 1930s and this very solid-looking Leyland Lion LT7 was purchased in April 1936. BAD 854 carried a thirty two-seat Duple body, and when photographed its headlights were fitted with wartime masks. One of its regular drivers, Mr Sidney Hunt, is seen with the vehicle. Mr Hunt had served with the RASC, but went to work for Warners when discharged on health grounds. In 1945 Cecil Warner died suddenly and his business was put on the open market. It was purchased by his brother Harold, who had continued to run the family business at Twyning. Harold was assisted in his new venture by his son Norman, and, following his demob, Norman's brother Charles. The business took the name of Warners Motors and went on to become a multi-faceted operation. Following a de-merger in 1981, Charles Warner continued with the coach operation and Norman took control of the various retail motor outlets in and around Tewkesbury and Gloucester. Both businesses continue to thrive today – the coach business is now in the hands of Charles' sons Richard and Nicholas, operating a number of local services in both Gloucestershire and Worcestershire, under the name of the Boomerang Bus Company. This Leyland served with Warners until 1954.

Bevan Brothers, trading as Soudley Valley Bus Services, began bus operations in 1929 with a Chevrolet and continued in business until 1998. The family was granted four wartime Bedford OWBs in order to maintain essential services.

A few vehicles which had been impressed for military service were actually released by the Ministry before the war was over. In a number of cases these were given new registration numbers, probably because the original documentation was not readily available. One such vehicle was this Bedford WTB, snapped up by Russell of Wormington. This 1936 vehicle, with Duple twenty-six-seat rear entrance coach body, was new to an operator by the name of Fancy in Portland, Dorset with registration JT 4140. When just a few months old, Southern National acquired the Fancy business and the Bedford received its new owner's green and cream livery. It was impressed by the military at the end of the decade, but released through an auction in Hampshire in 1944. The story is told that Mr Russell travelled to the sale by train, arriving back in Cheltenham at around 11 p.m. At that time of the evening there were no local trains or country buses, and Mr Russell chose to walk the fifteen or so miles back to his home with only the moon to provide illumination. Once recovered, he obtained registration FAD 827 for the vehicle, which he collected a few days later. It remained in service until sold in 1951 to Costelloe & Kemple, a Cheltenham contractor, who used it for staff transport for a further year. These photographs were taken just as the vehicle was about to leave the Russell fleet – by then beginning to show signs of a hard life.

The same bus, FAD 827, viewed from the front.

SCARROTT'S LUXURY COACHES.

Stow-on-the-Wold, Broadway and Evesham

SUMMER SERVICES commencing Wednesday, May 15th, 1940.

		Mondays p.m.	Wednes. p.m.	Fri. and Sats. p.m.	Fri. and Sats. p.m.	Sundays. p.m.	Sundays. p.m.
Icomb (War Memorial)	dep.	12-50		12-50	6-0	12-50	5-10
Westcote (Top) ...	,,	1-0		1-0	6-5	1-0	5-15
Rissington Aerodrome ...	,,	1-15	6-0	1-15	6-15	1-15	5-45
Stow-on-the-Wold (The Square)	,,	1-30	6-15	1-30	6-30	1-30	6-0
Upper Swell ...	,,	1-35		1-35	6-35	1-35	6-5
Condicote ...	,,	1-45		1-45	6-45	1-45	6-15
Longborough (The School)	,,	1-50	6-25	1-50	6-55	1-50	6-25
Broadway (The Clock)	,,	2-10	6-45	2-10	7-10	2-10	6-45
Evesham (Merstow Green)	arr.	2-30	7-0	2-30	7-30	2-30	7-0

		p.m.	p.m.	p.m.	p.m.	p.m.	p.m.
Evesham (Merstow Green)	dep.	6-0	10-30	4-40	10-30	3-0	10-15
Broadway (The Clock)	,,	6-15	10-45	4-55	10-45	3-15	10-30
Longborough (The School)	,,	6-35	11-5	5-20	11-5	3-40	10-50
Condicote ...	,,	6-45		5-30		3-50	11-0
Upper Swell ...	,,	6-50		5-40		3-55	11-10
Stow-on-the-Wold (The Square)	,,	6-55	11-15	5-45	11-15	4-0	11-15
Rissington Aerodrome ...	,,	7-10	11-30	6-0	11-30	5-10	11-30
Westcote (Top) ...	,,	7-15	11-35	6-5	11-35	5-15	11-35
Icomb (War Memorial)	arr.	7-20	11-40	6-15	11-40	5-20	11-40

```
Icomb
 2d.   —   Westcote
 4d.   6d.   —   —   Rissington Aerodrome
 6d.   9d.  6d.  9d.  6d.  9d.   Stow-on-the-Wold
 8d.   1/-  8d.  1/-  8d.  1/-  2d.   —   Upper Swell
10d.   1/2 10d.  1/2 10d.  1/2  5d.  9d.  3d.  5d.   Condicote
 1/-   1/4  1/-  1/4  1/-  1/4   —    —   6d. 10d.  3d.   —   Longborough
 1/6   2/-  1/6  2/-  1/6  2/-  1/2  1/9  1/-  1/6  1/-  1/6  10d.  1/4  Broadway
 1/9   2/6  1/9  2/6  1/9  2/6  1/6  2/-  1/6  2/-  1/4  1/9  1/4  1/9  Evesham
  S     R    S    R    S    R    S    R    S    R    S    R
        S—Single.    R—Return.
```

NOTE—Every endeavour will be made to run to the above times but the Proprietor does not hold himself responsible for any inconvenience caused.

Enquiries to C. SCARROTT, (Phone Stow 62)
Central Garage, STOW-ON-THE-WOLD.

Scarrott's of Stow on-the-Wold introduced this revised timetable for their service to Evesham for the summer of 1940.

Almost all vehicles so far illustrated are single-deckers, quite simply because double-deckers were virtually unknown among the independent operators in the pre-war years; indeed I believe that over the years the cumulative total never reached double figures. Two from Nailsworth are recorded in Chapter 4, three more are known to have operated in the 1920s with Norton Bros of Lechlade who used them on their route to Cirencester. In the early post-war years, Edwards of Lydbrook and Warners of Tewkesbury built up relatively significant numbers of double-deckers, and several other operators found it appropriate to include a few such vehicles in their fleets – but that is beyond the coverage of this volume. A.H. Kearsey Ltd of Cheltenham, however, began to acquire double-deckers just before wartime hostilities began. Their arrival was directly attributable to the much expanded work of the Gloster Aircraft Company at its various factories in the Brockworth area. Mr Arthur Kearsey was successful in obtaining the road service licences for transporting the many GAC workers from their homes around the Cheltenham area. Kearseys had started life at Staverton in around 1930 with a single Chevrolet, and by 1937 had built up to a fleet of some half dozen coaches. By the end of 1945, not only had the company moved to premises in Cheltenham, but a fleet of at least twenty-five vehicles was on the road, ten of which were double-deckers. It will be clear from the introductory remarks in this chapter that vehicle shortages at that time were acute, and to expand in this way could only be achieved by purchasing elderly vehicles which were being set aside by those operators lucky enough to be allocated new vehicles, or whose activities were being reduced. Most of the arrivals in the Kearsey fleet, single and double-deck, were well worn and much rebodying took place in order to match the better chassis with the least worn bodies to squeeze the last few years of service out of the resulting combinations. The wartime conditions resulted in few records being maintained of these rebuilds and virtually no photographs exist. Although these views of Kearsey vehicles were taken in the post-war years, they give a flavour of the company's war-time vehicles. JO 2385 was one of a pair of ten year old AEC Regents which Kearseys managed to acquire from City of Oxford Motor Services in 1940; both survived into the 1950s. The Regent is seen heading for Brockworth along Bath Road in Cheltenham to collect workers at the end of their shift.

Photographed at the same spot, three Kearsey double-deckers return from Brockworth; they appear to be empty and probably took the staff out at the start of the day. For all to be returning empty, rather than being parked at the factory with the drivers travelling back on a single vehicle, points to a relaxation of fuel rationing. Nearest the camera is one of four WH 33xx registered Leyland Titan TD1s dating from 1931, acquired from Bolton Corporation in 1939. At least three remained with Kearseys for a full decade. In front of it is AEC JO 2385 (see above).

GK 5718 was a Leyland Tiger TS3 dating from about 1930, but with a rather newer body. It arrived with Kearsey in 1943 after a short spell with Harvey of Chedworth, and moved on again in 1949.

DR 5806 was one of the first batch of AEC Regals ever produced; it was delivered to Plymouth Corporation along with eleven others in 1929. The vehicle had lost its original Mumford body when it arrived with Kearsey in 1945; it stayed until 1951. Once again it is seen heading for Brockworth. The photographs taken at the junction of Hermitage Street with Bath Road were taken by Mr Noel Meanwell, one of the few transport photographers in the town in the late 1940s.

Another Leyland Tiger to join the Kearsey fleet in 1943 was 1930 UU 1264, a TS2. The TS2 had a shorter wheelbase than the TS3, but both were built to conform to the then prevailing legal maximum vehicle length of 26ft. This TS2 kept an appointment with the scrapman in 1950.

For some years the smaller Leyland passenger model was the Cub, built at the Kingston (Surrey) plant. RN 7959 was a Cub SKPZ2, with a twenty-six-seat body and a relatively unusual centre door. It arrived in the Kearsey fleet in 1944 when about ten years old, and gave six years of service.

Although some pre-war coaches were impressed by the military, most continued to perform their daily duties, but excursion work was curtailed by fuel rationing. Fred Martin of Sling is thought to have bought this Commer Centaur new in 1934. It was fitted with a twenty-seat body by Jenkins of Harvington. The coach passed to Cox of Ellwood in November 1939 and Mr Cox is alongside in this view. In the doorway is his brother Ivor. The coach has its headlamp masks in position.

The only new double-decker supplied to a Gloucestershire independent operator during the war was a Daimler for Cottrells of Mitcheldean. This is the only known view of it with its original owner. It was registered FAD 657 and was a CWA6 model, with six-cylinder AEC engine. The body was by

Brush, and built to the lowbridge design, with a sunken upstairs gangway running to the side of the vehicle. Although this was the standard design for lowbridge vehicles until the mid-1950s, it was inconvenient for passengers and conductor alike. Upstairs passengers had to clamber into seats in rows of four bent almost double under the restricted headroom; those on the offside of the lower deck had to duck when leaving their seats as the upstairs gangway intruded into the lower deck roof space. The vehicle moved on to Kearsey of Cheltenham in 1957 and continued in use for a further three years.